The Cosmic Egg

Fritz Blackburn

Published by Fritz Blackburn, 2024.

While every precaution has been taken in the preparation of this book, the publisher assumes no responsibility for errors or omissions, or for damages resulting from the use of the information contained herein.

THE COSMIC EGG

First edition. July 27, 2024.

Copyright © 2024 Fritz Blackburn.

ISBN: 979-8227665010

Written by Fritz Blackburn.

Table of Contents

The Cosmic Egg

The complete theory of a living universe and everything
By Fritz Blackburn
Copyright © 2016 Fritz Blackburn

INTRODUCTION

Do we still care, in today's confused world, about why the universe exists, where it came from, what it may become, and why we ourselves exist inside this immense, seemingly empty cosmos? Have we given up on what we think is unsolvable, or do we just placidly leave those things to the physicists, the 'specialists', like everything else? Have market values and consumerism suffocated those questions of ages-old existential importance, without which we would still sit in the trees, eating bananas? Do we want to know why we are, who we are, what reality really is? Does the modern reader want to be entertained and excited only, or is she capable of passion for the ultimate truth, the larger picture? Can she accept the possible loss of her entire worldview when faced with the truth?

To read and fully understand what follows—we need to be ready to change, to let go of illusion and prejudice, and to take personal responsibility.

Only a deprogrammed brain, an 'empty' mind, as the Taoists call it, can see clearly enough beyond its time, its cultural and scientific prejudices and limitations.

This presented theory of everything is originally based on vision, but it is committed to the language, method, and outlook of contemporary physics. It elegantly solves the chicken/egg riddle of where the universe originally came from and explains the Creation event in terms of the mechanics of form, a concept astonishingly overlooked by physics since Plato.

As, according to quantum mechanics, any act of observation changes the observed event, the scientist himself, who attempts to understand, and also the reader of his theory). He needs to become a complete observer—one that is not limited by specialization, by any divisive attempt at 'objectivity' at the expense of personal experience, or by culturally established worldviews and so-called 'facts'. The witness needs to practice 'complete observation', accept and cultivate his personal involvement when experiencing reality, and see the connections as much as the differences. Objective verification comes later!

From such a state of mind only can we gain enough clarity to discover that all the necessary puzzle-pieces, needed to relate the universe to the existence of life and to the four physical forces, and to explain all phenomena in a single theory—have long been available! It can be completely understood where this universe originally came from, where 'evolution' inevitably leads, and - how the universe accounts for the appearance of the human form inside its seemingly mechanistic structure!

Since simplicity is the best measure for ultimate truth, all things must be explainable in terms of basic and obvious principles. And those basic principles, as can be comprehended by a non-physicist, hold indeed the key to the self-perpetuating design of Creation and life—and to the four forces of physics, which can in this way be related.

It can be demonstrated that the universe has to be a living thing that man existed long before the universe started to evolve—and we can now become aware of what this so-called 'God' , that mankind has consistently evoked throughout history and cultures, is really all about.

Einstein's theory of relativity can be extended and proves far more general and conclusive than he himself had ever expected—once it includes the relativity given by the relative size of the observer!

The explanation given is not tainted by any religious belief system not held by the author, nor is it in any way vague, limited, mystical or unverifiable. It simply picks up the relevant puzzle-pieces—and puts them together the only way they can possibly fit - and where the whole picture is recognized as inevitable.

A complete, or even peripheral mathematical elaboration would have stretched the author's qualifications, and it would defeat the purpose of intelligibly grasping an entirely new paradigm of reality by the non-specialized and simple intelligent reader. Enough mathematical details are, however, given to allow the serious physicist vast opportunities for testing and verification of the concept outlined.

The scope of this theory ensures that the biologist will be as astounded as the cosmologist—as it reveals the secrets of genetics to be of the ultimate cosmological relevance. The so-called laws of nature are shown to conduct a 'mechanics of form'; they are but dualistic aspects of more general principles that determine reality.

All the puzzle pieces we have collected in the various disciplines fit with uncanny precision the interconnected and complete picture that inexorably reveals itself. The answers are easy to find; the problem was always that we never asked just the right question! And the ancient questions about evolution, the existence of life, even about alien life, that we thought could only ever lead to new questions and defy definite answers, are for the first time answered conclusively by the mechanics of form and by a model of the living universe that for good reason cannot help but create human beings!

The stunning conclusion to the known interconnected facts of life is—that 'God' is not metaphysical at all, but physical and female, that biology and physics are only differentiated by the size of the observer, and that this universe contains the human form in order to have a reason to expand...

This is a sober attempt at translating visionary realization of what the universe really is into verifiable theorem; to build that bridge between polar opposites—in order to arrive at the One that explains all of the many.

There is much value in the humbling insight of how small we are in the face of universal vastness and intelligence, and it is without doubt vital for us to realize how little we really know. But the opposite is equally true! In a fractal universe, where the whole is contained in its smallest part, the All can be fully recognized by its smallest parts! For this reason, we can actually understand the universe and tap into this absolute knowledge far beyond our own experience.

It is quite possible to access those unused ninety percent of our brains, and even DNA itself, when certain realizations and connections are made, and certain inner technique employed by an observer observing himself first!

This book presents a totally unifying theory of physics and everything, but it also has a powerfully mind-expanding, therapeutic effect on the reader. It can indeed free the mind from dualistic illusion, teach truly relativistic thinking and observation, and lead through the conflicting paradoxes of our divided world views to the Oneness of Form—and to actual insight into who we really are.

1. Five-dimensional Space

God is in the details, certainly, but the recognition of God is in relating all those details to Oneness! Conventional science, in its fragmented and analytical approach to observation, uses mostly the left, rational side of the brain. Feeling, intuition, and participation are not part of 'pure' science. If, however, the whole is mirrored as fractals by its parts, then the parts, including mankind, have to carry in themselves the potential of conceiving of the whole, and need to apply this fractal awareness as a method to perceive wholeness. To identify with left or right is the classic, debilitating mistake of humans! We need to see left and right, and any other pair of opposites, not as an either/or decision, but as Oneness, as an orientation for free choice. Left without right is fundamentally non-existent and intrinsically meaningless, in physics as in politics and anywhere. If the scientist applies such basic truths of life and nature to his own practical approach, he will use the left **and** the right side of his brain, rather than deciding on the limited options of following either logic or intuition, and either objective non-participation or subjective self-projection. There is no 'perfect' concept, and no right way for anything. The training of a cosmogonist therefore needs to include many other subjects, and guide to insights that allow her to become truly unprejudiced, truly untainted by her time and culture, religion, gender or skin colour!

Is it not obvious? —a holistic question can only be answered by a holistic observer. A physicist must also be a philosopher, a biologist, a spiritually aware being who always looks at both sides of any coin. In the light of such balance, the question of whether the universe is comprehensible appears to be only half the question! The other half is—can the universe be intuited by man? This kind of wholeness in questions is a necessary requirement to finding unification and the theory of every-thing! She, the 'objective' observer needs to also become a subjective participant! With a little practice, we will discover that every law of nature, every observable form, and every physical truth is a perfect mirror image of a corresponding mental or spiritual reality in humans—no matter how much objective verification we add to personal observation. In the stone age, it was generally understood by people that the cave bear, the lion, the lizard, and the eagle, were parts of their own spirits—totems, as the native Americans call them. Animals and plants are indeed part of a collective human Mind, part of a shared common subconscious.

The world is our perfect mirror, our own creation, and everything we see reminds us of who we are. All physical laws and observations seem to have a counterpart in our souls and psyches. We could just by knowing ourselves, deduce every physical law there is to discover, from our own mind/body.

As an example may serve the intimation of the dimensions from our bodies:

Our hand gives us five dimensions, as do our feet, and we have five outward-orientated senses, which is five-dimensional sensing of the world!

Space is also five-dimensional

This is not to say, there are no other 'dimensions' to space or mind-space, like dream space-time (astral projection) or parallel realities, states of enlightenment. What is meant is that any materially defined human view of space is perfectly described by five dimensions!

Space is generally understood only as three-dimensional:

It has—length, width and height.

Then there is allegedly a temporal dimension, which seems to add a fourth dimension (when applied in a certain frame of reference).

The truth is much less arbitrary—let us look at the underlying dualities of length, width and height to understand what and why they are:

1. Forward and backward (length)
2. Left and right (width)
3. Up and down (height)

The spiritual and the day by day existential experience of man has exactly the same orientations! His path goes forward and backward, left and right, up and down. His mind, spirit and body have the same dimensions—he is running forward or thrown back; he is right or not, not only walks, but also feels and looks up or down. Once we see the symmetries between the outer and the inner world, it becomes much clearer just how many, and which, dimensions there really are.

There are five elements and five basic dimensions to space inside this universe.

Those five orientations are mental, spiritual and physical dimensions of the human condition—and of physics!

1. Forward / backward
2. Left / right
3. Up / down
4. Clockwise /Anticlockwise
5. Inside/outside

Without the fourth and the fifth dimension, this universe cannot be described beyond our present physics! Time is not, as Einstein thought, a dimension of its own! It belongs partly to all five dimensions, but mostly to the human mind. The past/future is an aspect of forward/backward, and of the movements of sun, moon and stars, which define 'time' as clock/anticlockwise spin. Time is not a dimension; it only seems to be. Time is another way to say space or movement. It is an illusion projected by our own changing states of mind and it certainly does not exist as one of the five spatial dimensions.

The fourth dimension—

is given by the rotation of all building blocks of nature either in an anti-clockwise-wise or clockwise direction, whether they are atoms, planets, stars, galaxies or galactic clusters! Of course, the illusion of time is related to the fourth dimension: If the earth suddenly turned the other way around, the early morning would turn straight back into night and into yesterday. Time would begin to run backwards. A galaxy spinning clockwise would, relative to our Milky Way, which spins anti-clockwise, run from our future to our past, sending out particles which run backwards in time. Vortex is in principal a 'time machine' —and time an illusion created by the observer trapped by counting its spin, and not knowing why it spins. We run in circles, because we don't discover the connecting spiral, and that space is curved not by time but by form—and by spin.

To understand the deeper nature of vortex, it is again necessary to look within: The human form on its energetic level consists entirely of such vortex clusters, the strongest of which make up its nine energy centers, the chakras.

The human experience is determined by how active these chakras are, and which way they are spinning. The yogic system and all other esoteric systems in the world know these energy-centers, which behave like turning energy-wheels, like inner spiral galaxies. On a denser level of perception, medicine calls these chakras 'endocrine glands.'

Finally, the universal structure at its constituent levels is spiral. Matter is organized as a looping double helix. The spiral (vortex + vertical vector) arises geometrically from the vectors given by the first three dimensions:

Forward + Right + Up = rising clockwise spiral.

The function of spiral and vortex (flat spiral) is the bending of space from the inside of a hierarchical box into the outside—and vice versa!

Cosmic space is not as homogeneous or as continuous as it seems from our planetary perspective, even if a time factor is used to explain it. Space consists in hierarchical boxes within larger boxes, and as soon as the observer within any box tries to describe space outside his box and of the universe at large, he cannot do this without the

fifth dimension—inside/outside!

The physical laws inside a galaxy are one thing, but the laws outside quite another. This is why space travel cannot work in a linear way, cannot continue in the same way outside this galaxy. Space travel has to consider hierarchical quantum jumps from box to larger box. This can be understood more easily when a far better-known universe, like our own body, is observed. Human beings experience the inside of their bodies as greatly different from the outside! Medically, we can explain this away by the nerves inside the body, and no nerves outside. Spiritually it is of course also possible to feel cut off from the outside in a way where we don't feel the pain of others, or let their happiness not reach our own hearts. It is always possible to explain this with nerves and boundaries, but in reality, we're just stuck either inside ourselves, or stuck in the world outside—in an either/or situation! This kind of blindness is the 'original sin' in physics, in politics, in ecology, in philosophy, in relationships, in sex—everywhere!

It is impossible to differentiate at all between physical or spiritual laws, because body, mind and spirit are not three different things, only three ways of looking at one and the same thing.

Let's take an architect's house for example: It is complete, furnished and landscaped in his mind, long before it escapes those confinements of micro-space and grows into the 'real' world of our planetary scale. The house, nobody will doubt that, will once it is built and finished, have vastly different spatial co-ordinates from the same house in the micro-spatial (chemical) visualization processes in the architect's brain, which is just as real! The micro- manifestation of the house is symmetrical to its outside manifestation, the difference being only one of hierarchical scale and of location inside and outside of the observer. The design of the house (its inner structure) is of course a projection of the emotional, mental and spiritual state of the architect—an idea—but the house, visualized in every detail, is just as physically and chemically real in the microcosm of the brain...

The inside/outside is the dimension responsible for the contracting and the expanding force. **If there were no outside to this universe, it could not expand!** The inside strives to become its opposite, so it expands and grows. The outside wants to get inside, and contracts itself into micro-space. It is the ultimate generalization, since all things behave like that on all levels. This explains the psychology of sex, the technology of plumbing, the four physical forces, and the mechanics of all form. As the inside/outside is a physical dimension, it is also a dimension of the human mind, and of equally fundamental importance to psychotherapy. We're all either withdrawn to the inside (introverted)—or stuck at the outside (extroverted or superficial). Autism is the classic Gestalt of being trapped inside. The average lawyer, businessman or politician is trapped on the outside, which is just as blinding, but accepted by our social philosophies. The only healing for this constant error consists in learning to switch between the opposites as a first step, and then live them simultaneously, without any conflict of either-or.

The seed needs to be conscious of the tree it will become, and the tree needs to be conscious of the seed it develops. Human beings can talk and express more easily after sufficient listening and observing, and by expressing ourselves we can be more at ease in our inner silence.

The truth is very simple: At birth, we move from the inside to the outside, which is the most dramatic and awful experience in every life. Then we open our eyes and ears, and the world rushes in—all the forms and all sound enter our inside. Then we start talking, expressing, eating and defecating, and then starts puberty, where we contract our form onto the genetic level of sperm and egg, and think of little beside penetration into the inside and being penetrated by the outside. This is what a genuine law of nature looks like: it applies not only to physics, or genetics or the economy, but to every sense and each experience. Similarly, the physical laws (like gravitation) and the conditions within a living cell are vastly different from outside that cell. The conventional laws do not really cease to apply in the intra-cellular space, but the law of gravitation and the behaviour of light inside a cell need to be seen in the light of inside/outside relativity to make any sense. The difference between quantum physics and biology lies entirely with this hierarchical inside/outside, where one describes the atomic space and the other the cellular space.

A mouse can be described by the quantum physicist as a universe of quantum phenomena, by the biologist as a form observed on a parallel biological plane, and by the mouse herself as an inner energetic reality of self-feelings. Looking from all these positions is applied relativity, in a scientific and spiritual sense. It is objective/subjective observation of inner/outer reality. Conventional, non-hierarchical physics may conceive only of parallel realities, like far away suns and planets of our own 'box' (galaxy), not however of a reality which is outside, that is hierarchically above our spatial vessel, the Milky Way. Galactic space, like atomic or cellular space is fundamentally beyond our planetary physics, and the reason for this is the dimension of inside/outside given by the hierarchical structure of our mind/space universe. Spiritually, to be trapped inside or outside makes oneness impossible, and the All invisible.

The dimensions of our universe are like our spiritual path, and as on any path—one step, two steps, three steps—we walk the path of creation! Until we come to a crossroad and to the implied decision of turning left or right. The enlightened master can still turn left and right, walk the paddock, sit down, turn around, according to the motto—if you get to a fork in the road—take it! Yet most of us will decide left or right, halving and unbalancing reality.

The next thing sure to happen is that our path will go uphill and downhill. As long as it all goes up we are happy, but when we go downhill we get depressed (if we dislike walking this can reverse). The master enjoys the entire walk...

Most people have only ever experienced walking three-dimensionally. The fourth dimension requires conscious activation of our energy-centers, and a non-linear mental state. It is then possible for man to experience the spiral, the implosion of form from the outside onto his inner awareness via what we can call harmonics!

The fifth dimension then—takes us out of the box we are in!

The inside comes out and the cosmic harmonics are allowed in. This is the physical definition of the enlightened state where the illusion of an individual, separate existence ceases, and we are entering the next dimension. We will further define the inside/out in the terms of physics when we examine the structure of the universe in the chapters on hierarchy. What we find is that spatial and mental hierarchy are identical, just as body and mind are identical. Creation and creator are also one and the same, and so are seed and tree, man and God.

2. Form and hierarchy

While light, color and the various properties of matter; like weight, temperature, size, and texture are all considered physical realities and have been well explored mathematically, there is one quality of the same physical phenomena, which is so little understood that it has never found a place in the natural sciences. This quality is what we commonly call—form.

The Greek philosophers, who were also great natural scientists, saw the forms as ideas, that is as belonging to the metaphysical world. Nevertheless, the forms are something we constantly meet in our every-day experience, and the form of a thing is the first and the strongest quality of every object we encounter.

In physics, we are asking questions like: What is the smallest building block of nature—or, what is the nature of the universe—which are questions pointing at the nature of form. Since however form cannot, it seems, be quantified, or dealt with mathematically, it has been widely ignored and left out of consideration within the physical theories on reality.

Since Darwin, form has become even less significant, as the forms of life are seen as the chance product of a random evolution, determined by environment and by the survival of the fittest. The generally accepted idea that form is not conserved contributes to the doubts over its physical reality as much as our inability to discern according to what design it develops.

Still, we recognize all things by their form, and at the root of quantum physics we cannot decide, whether the universe is built from solid particles or from waves, which brings us back to the original question of what form really is.

Can something take the form of a wave and of a solid object at the same time, or is form beyond the physical aspects of reality and but a consequence of the method we use to look at things? Is form physically real or only an idea which is unrelated to the physical world?

These questions seem to mark the core of the scientific difficulty to come to a conclusive understanding of nature since the early attempts of the Greek two-and-a-half-thousand years ago.

In our time, when we have described the phenomena and analyzed their composite parts to some extent, we have arrived at a measure of specialization, where the parts must be put together again in order to discover the Whole.

We now want to know, what exactly the universe is, what purpose or function it has, and where its design comes from.

In as much as any design is the smaller version of the final form, quantum physics and cosmology alike will now have to face the question of form and its relationship to design! The form of the universe and the design of it are what brings cosmology and quantum physics together. This is the basic realization needed to unify these two loose ends of physics, and only when form is understood in terms of design can the forces and the phenomena be interrelated.

Before we can explore the mechanics of form in a way that will make form accessible to mathematical reason, we will first need to take a fresh and unprejudiced look at how form as such is organized in a universe as it is described by modern physics.

The evolution of astrophysics and cosmology started with an experience shared by every human being on Earth who could look up at the sky and see the sun, the moon and the stars! This experience, touching the human soul with awe and mystery, shaped the cosmological questions we are still trying to solve today.

The perspective given by the celestial bodies seems strangely different from the arrangement of phenomena on the surface of the planet Earth. All of nature on Earth is interconnected in the multiple cycles of causal relationships that make it impossible for any part to exist without the other parts. Vegetation grows from the soil and returns to the soil. Animals live from vegetation and also disintegrate into the soil. Human beings depend on both plants and animals, and they share the same needs for water, sunlight and shelter. Everything is interrelated and moves in cycles, and everything is an aspect of the common principles of fire, water, earth, air and life. However, all forms on Earth are members of the same reality and scale, subject to the same physical forces, and they exist parallel to each other. The complexity of form and its variety and multitude make it difficult to see the interwoven cyclical network of the whole system, commonly experienced as nature. To our senses, nature is a complexity of parallel forms, and form itself is consequently seen as a haphazard product of a random evolution and the physical forces. The existence of celestial bodies like the moon and the stars seem to break this pattern and give us a sense of apartness, of vastness and of lifelessness. We feel the limitations of our scale when we can't reach the stars, and we are mystified about the possible connections they may have with us since we know only a nature of interconnectedness...

It is easy to be humble and objective enough to admit that nature on a cosmic scale does not necessarily continue the patterns we can observe on Earth, like the existence of life, the cyclical movements of the five elements, and the existence of consciousness. Thus, we have come to consider humankind and every form we know as uniquely confined to this planet, and our separate reality as a freak of evolution or a whim of God.

Even today, knowing the stars to be suns like our own, and part of entire galaxies of stars, the mystery remains despite or because of the quantitative and mechanistic explanations offered by a science trying to satisfy our need to make sense of the unknown in terms of solid matter, size, charge, distance or chemical change.

The main reason for our inability to relate to the forms of macro-cosmic scale is however a principle in nature that arranges form beyond the range of the human senses, which are tuned to only this scale, and in an entirely different way from what our mind is conditioned to—forms from macro-cosmic space down to microcosmic space are hierarchically organized!

The sun, the moon and the stars have for millennia been nothing but form and light to the human observer. The sun worshipers, the moonlight walkers, and the stargazers were all equally enthralled by a simple spherical shape that stood like the word of God written in the sky—a statement of nature for every observer to read, to contemplate and to form his metaphysical ideas from. Nothing has motivated human consciousness and curiosity as much as the spheres of the heavens—to seek form beyond our earthly scale.

Astronomy, which lies at the beginning of all science, grew from the celestial spheres and so did poetry and the sense of something higher than ourselves, which gives us direction for intellectual growth and scope for awareness.

Form and light are the two most forming and enlightening principles that have made humankind capable of recognition, and form, light will continue to be the principal guides of a science intent to solve the puzzle of existence.

The properties of matter like mass, quantity size or weight, which occupy modern physics cannot answer the mystery introduced by form. It has to be understood that form is not a property of matter, even if form can materialize.

This can be simply proven by visualizing form independently of the presence of its materialized manifestation. Television does the same thing by transporting the form of a politician over a distance without having to carry the body along. Form is therefore not necessarily a product of the physical universe. If form has such a unique position in nature and in the evolution of human thought, it cannot be ignored in the context of the origin of the physical forces and of the 'first move.'

Gravity may evolve the celestial spherical forms, but does gravity also cause the parachutist? And where was gravity, when the universe was born from the first particle? The form of any first particle was certainly not created by gravity.

The universe, created by a God or not, repeats the spherical form throughout the hierarchy. This form of the sphere is the alignment of matter particles that try to move as close to each other as possible. We call this gravitation. However, the force of gravitation cannot create the first sphere! The human form also cannot be designed by the forces, or by random evolution, particularly not the individual human form. It is, at least as far as we can observe, passed down hierarchically from the large to the small through reproduction and genetics.

It can however be structurally reduced as consisting entirely of tiny spheres, which we call atoms on one level, or cells on a higher level of the hierarchy. Even when the human form disintegrates, and when it becomes difficult to see the shape of the human body, the atomic spheres will continue their life-cycles and will be used by other forms to evolve towards a higher level than their own.

It is indeed the most urgent purpose of nature to repeat form on various levels of scale, growing from the small towards the big.

The planets of our solar system are all dedicated witnesses and performers of this dance of the spheres around another larger sphere, which is again part of a greater sphere which is the Milky Way galaxy. Since all spheres are contained in each other, we can speak of a 'Chinese box-in-a-box' system, which describes the fundamental principle of nature to organize form hierarchically from microcosmic minimum to macro-cosmic maximum. The resulting hierarchy of scale is an organization that is unexplainable by the physical forces and it will need to be understood as the basic spatial design, before the forces can be interrelated.

The hierarchical ladder of nature stretches at least from the smallest building block known to man, which is the nucleus of the atom, to the largest knowable macro-cosmic scale, which is the universe. The quarks, more energy than material, are just outside this hierarchy of material building-blocks. The hierarchy also comprises the obviously organic levels of organization, of which the human form is an evolved example.

The levels of the hierarchy are therefore given as follows:

Universe
Super-cluster
Cluster
Galaxy
Solar System
Planet
Organisms
Cell
Atom
Nucleon

It is assumed by cosmology, that there is nothing outside this universe, and that there is nothing smaller than the quark. This may be correct as far as the hierarchical range of the observable, materially definable universe is concerned, which may be a complete unit in itself. It does however not allow a logical conclusion that the universe is the only such form and does not know a parallel or a hierarchical existence of form beyond itself.

The question of an end to the continuity of the hierarchical organization will depend on the evolutionary stage of forms and can to be left open at this stage.

As far as the known range of the hierarchy is concerned, it appears to have a direction, which is the evolution from the small units towards bigger units. The movement into this direction serves the purpose of repeating form on larger levels

We must not forget, of course, that the hierarchy of forms is not sterile and absolute, but contains this interesting structural detail: In between the atomic level and the planetary level, the hierarchy produces clearly discernible organismic levels, organized from organic molecules to form cells, organelles, organs and organisms. At least on this planet we can observe these levels to be part of the hierarchy.

As far as we can see, this organic level is not needed for the evolution of the larger macro-cosmic levels in which it is contained. The underlying purpose of nature, if the existence of the observer is not to be ascribed to coincidence, seems to be therefore to produce these forms of the organic level for their own sake and not as necessary building-blocks for the higher, 'inorganic,' levels of those macro-cosmic spheres!

If the universe follows the austerely simple method of repeating form and of hierarchical continuation throughout its range, we must ask where the design of the organic levels comes from, where it is repeated and how the human existence fits into the hierarchical or fractal pattern of which it undeniably is a part.

This in mind, we need to take a fresh look at the observable levels and decide whether they do indeed constitute separate realities of a mechanistic, haphazard nature of less purpose than we would have imagined, or whether they relate to the human existence as the ancients thought, and as our senses make us feel in a starlit night.

3. The planetary level

Of the countless things that could be said about the planet Earth, there are only three characteristics of particular interest in the context of the planet's position within the hierarchy.

The first basic characteristic of the Earth is the fact, that it is a sphere. What we take for granted today was rightfully considered a revolutionary discovery in the time of Copernicus.

As it always happens once a new idea becomes well-established fact, it ceases soon to be a miracle. By giving the mechanistic causes for the roundness of celestial bodies, science has lost the appreciation for the fact as such. If we find it difficult to understand the why and how of creation in its variety of forms, would it not be a simplified mathematical task to start with the genesis of the sphere? Does not the form of this planet influence and determine each and every thing we know, including our own existence?

The sphere is defined as equal expansion in all directions from a point. It is the classic no-form, symbolic of the number one.

The simple sphere creates all the other forms all by itself! It divides, and thus becomes two and four and eight. Three equal spheres, trying to be as intimately close as possible, will create a triangle between their heavy centers and their energies. Four spheres form a tetrahedron, six spheres make an octahedron, eight spheres a dice, twelve spheres form an icosahedron—just by moving together as close as possible! The many are implicit in and organized by—the One. Given the form of the sphere and the attraction between spheres, the creation of all matter and of mathematics is implicit.

At this stage, it may suffice to simply be aware of the spherical form of our home planet as the largest reality to the human eye, having a rotation in which we participate.

The second characteristic of Earth is its participation in a larger system. Earth is not an isolated entity in space, but a member of much larger systems. The coexistence of the planets with the sun is one of harmony, of well-established distances, and of a subtle connection. The harmonious cyclical principles found on Earth are repeated by the behaviour of the planet as a whole, in relation to the sun.

And the third characteristic is that Earth is alive! Just like any organism, this planet consists mostly of what science would call 'dead matter,' but this quantitative consideration is completely meaningless in the face of all known forms of life being a part of Earth!

This may seem a mere philosophical statement to some, but it is really a fundamental, if quite ignored, right-brain realization and the only qualitative foundation of a healthy scientific framework.

Humans do not actually realize that they are part and expression of the Earth itself. We emphasize our own life, and along with it the use and the advantages received from Earth, like food and fuel. We focus much less on the fact that we will give it all back when we disintegrate to join the Earth again!

Unfortunately, any gratitude for receiving all and everything we need from the Earth, has been replaced by an attitude of excessive taking, which technology takes to its most extreme. This change, produced by the philosophies of materialism and consumerism and the greed of people feeling no longer part of nature, has destroyed all awareness for a balanced and mature oneness with the Earth which is our very substance.

By destroying the Earth, we naturally destroy ourselves as well as our ability to have a science capable of relating the human existence to the Earth, which has become an object.

If our self-projected errors are taken away from pure observation, what remains is the Oneness of all the parts of the Earth, and a recognition of the absurdity to distinguish categorically between the 'dead' matter of the Earth and the life forms to which it assembles.

In truth, everything on Earth is a quality and an expression of the planet itself, which must be defined as a living organism—because a Whole cannot possibly be less alive than any of its parts!

Even the motor-car is of course a natural expression of Earth! Just like the silk Chinese worms produce, or bee-hives. Plastic is a natural product, since Nature produced man—and man then made plastic!

Physically, every rock will one day become fine soil, used by plants, eaten by animals and humans. Each mineral in our bodies was at some stage a rock, and a piece of the primeval fireball. One must beware of taking this as a mere philosophical idea! The living Earth is a most fundamental axiom on which we need to base a physical science capable of producing real results!

All life-forms on Earth celebrate the life of the Earth as a whole, and have no separate existence of their own. For this reason, the Earth has been considered a Goddess of creation in the past, and still today many natural people identify the Earth with Gaia, the living Earth Mother, who brings forth all life.

4. The solar level

The Earth is a building block of the solar system, of which the sun is the centre. While this planet is not necessary to constitute the larger system, all the planets together are needed to give the solar system its characteristic function.

The sun by itself could exist without any planets, as far as its quantitative existence is concerned, but it would not be able to evolve its inherent qualities, such as the ability to use its energy to create the forms of life it has produced by having planets.

The existence of planets is not explained by gravity as a causal factor, because the stability gravity is striving for, can be achieved by condensing all available matter into the sun alone. The theories explaining how gravity forms a star plus satellites, do not give a reason why stars regularly evolve to systems with satellites in their orbits. An investigation into this phenomenon will show that the probabilities given by gravity do not account for the evolution of such systems.

Like Earth, the sun is a sphere, but the solar system as a whole is a rotating disk, where (almost!) all the planets orbit the sun in the same direction and on the same plane. The rotation of the planets around the sun is as much explainable by gravity and initial angular momentum, as it is by the form of the sphere, which 'curves' the space around it. The cyclical movement can be considered an inherent quality of the spherical form, and what the planets really do is to follow the pattern given by the spherical form of the sun, since this large sphere creates the geometrical law in the space it dominates.

The fact and the direction of the rotation give a spherical system the appearance of a disk, which implies that form and movement in a direction influence each other. This observation is necessary to understand the evolution of form in general, as will be shown later.

Cosmology has accumulated much detailed knowledge about the sun, as far as weight, age, distance, heat and the fusion of atoms are concerned.

Regarding the functional position of the stars within the hierarchy as a whole and the sun's relation to humankind, little qualitative progress has been achieved, since the sun is now seen as a machine-like furnace like the billions of other (useless) stars. The life-giving qualities of the sun are explained as coincidental, rather than as intrinsic, and life itself is not understood to be a function of the sun's inherent properties.

If we don't get distracted for a moment by what we know quantitatively about the sun, and instead look at it in an act of pure observation, as humans could naturally do throughout evolution, we can become aware of a simple but essential fact: the sun has only two objective qualities it conveys to the human observer to make of them what he will. These two qualities may well account for every qualitative aspect we will ever derive from telescopes and from mathematical interpretations. These two essential qualities are—Form and Light! The sun is nothing but form and light to the observer hoping to understand the universe by understanding its observable parts!

While the spherical shape of the sun is repeated throughout the hierarchical organization, the phenomenon of light seems to be a property of the stars alone. In order to understand the essence of what the sun really is, beyond the mechanistic and technological limitations of 21st century science, we have to comprehend the Nature of light.

Light, as Maxwell showed, is only a tiny band in a continuous spectrum. The difference between radiations that we can see, and radiations that we cannot see—so dramatic to the human eye—is only a few manometers of wave length. Why is it that this tiny portion of the electromagnetic spectrum is responsible for vision, for the rhythmic day-night regulations of many biological activities, for the bending of plants toward the light and also for photosynthesis, on which life depends? Is it an amazing coincidence that all the biological activities depend on the same wave lengths?

George Wald of Harvard, an expert on the subjects of light and life, said no—life can only exist on the planetary level of the Earth, dependent on exactly the wave lengths given as they are. Radiations of even slightly higher energies than the energy of violet light breaks the bonds of hydrogen and other weak bonds, and so disrupts the structure and function of the molecules. Radiation with wave lengths less than 200 nanometers—that is, with still higher energies—is absorbed by water, which makes up the great bulk of all living things on Earth.

When this light is absorbed by molecules, its lower energy causes them to increase their motion (increasing heat) but does not trigger changes in their electron configurations. Only those radiations within the range of visible light have the property of exciting molecules that is, of moving electrons into higher energy levels and so of producing chemical and, ultimately, biological changes.

The second reason that the visible band of the electromagnetic spectrum has been chosen by things, so goes the theory, is that it is what is available. Most of the radiation reaching the surface of the Earth from the sun is within this range. It can be noted, that exactly the wave lengths that are relevant to life on Earth, are also the visible spectrum, which suggests, that the essential qualities of Nature are also the most visible ones, as if we were supposed to see the important rather than the unimportant. Unless everything is random! Indeed, as we will see, the qualities of form and light that we can observe with the naked eye, describe the essential nature of the sun much better than all the other 'laws' as deduced by aided vision and by analysis.

It is after all the sun's light which alone transmits every bit of information about the sun to the human observer! The spectral lines alone hold amazing quantities of information: the speed of a star moving towards or away from the solar system, the rapidity of a star's rotation, the temperature of its surface, the strength of its magnetic field, even the amount of gas that is drifting in space between it and the Earth.

If light is the only actual source of information about the sun, it has to contain every single quality of the sun in its code of wave lengths, that is then translated back by the human eye and the mind, to derive a visualization of what we then call the 'sun.'

Whereas the sun itself is too remote to encounter as an immediate reality, it is only the light that we can ever meet, and it is light alone on which we base all our cosmological speculations. Since light contains all we know about the sun, it has to be more than just a product of the sun, or a by-product of the sun's activities.

In reality, light is not at all a property of the sun or of the solar system, and it is not limited to any level of the hierarchy. Light can actually only be understood in terms of the atomic theory and ultimately by the concept of form!

Each element—or kind of atom—can emit and absorb energy only at the specific wave lengths dictated by its atomic structure! In the spectrum of incandescent gas, the bright lines are produced by atoms emitting energy at their predetermined wave lengths. In the spectrum of the sun, the dark lines are produced by the action of elements in the solar atmosphere that absorbs radiation at their prescribed wave lengths.

If an electron is knocked all the way out of an atom by a gamma-ray quantum, after being close to the atom's nucleus, it usually gives rise to an X-ray. An electron that is almost but not quite knocked out of an atom (hurled, say from a close orbit to a remote one) usually gets rid of its unwanted energy in the form of ultraviolet rays.

Electrons which have been jolted only a few orbits outwards generally give off the sort of radiation that we know as visible light—still smaller electron jumps can produce the even longer rays of infra-red, commonly known as heat. Each element's distinctive kind of atom has its own private sending and receiving wave lengths corresponding to the pattern of its few or many orbiting electrons.

Light can therefore be defined as a function of the atomic system. Since atoms are older than the stars, the light contained in the atom is not caused, but only released, by the fusion processes of the younger stars. Light is inseparably linked to form. Not only does form determine light, as with the atomic structure, but light also transports form across space, be it the forms transmitted by television or the form of a tree transmitted to the human eye, or the celestial forms communicating their existence throughout space.

The form of the sun is transported by light and this is why we know of the form of the sun. So, it is the form of the atom that makes the form of the sun known to us! Since the sun and the atom have spherical rotating form, we can say, that light is the means of the spherical form to communicate itself, to copy and reproduce itself throughout the hierarchy. In order to make sense of the hierarchical structure and the true nature of the universe, it is essential to understand light as the transporting agent of form, as determined by form and as the agent of change of form. Most important to us humans, light triggers the evolution of life by triggering molecular change. Logic therefore tells us that evolution is predetermined by the atomic structure or by preexisting forms generally. This observation will have to be at the root of a new understanding of the evolution of life in terms of the hierarchy of forms.

The rotating motions of the solar system are also observable to humans with the naked eye. Rotation is movement dictated by the form and the qualities of the sphere. The cyclical principle is, as much as light, an essential ingredient of life where the cycles of day and night, of the seasons, the water cycle, and the life cycle itself constitute the movements of change, necessary for growth and continuation.

Our perception of 'time' is due entirely to the cyclical movements of the solar system, and could otherwise hardly exist. Also, our perspective of the small and the vast, the whole idea of space has been shaped by this cyclical system that gives us intermediate bodies of larger size, connecting the scales on Earth with the tiny dots of the far away stars, which are really bigger than we could have ever guessed.

The bodies of the solar system alone have given humans a hint of the hierarchy. If the naked eye had never seen the sun or the moon, the human mind would have had no reason to look for atoms or galaxies or any other building stone of an unsuspected universe. It seems that the sun has not only provided for the ingredients of physical life, but offers all the necessary information as well, for an intelligent consciousness to become aware of the larger realities.

The existence of the planets beside our own, in the same system, has more than anything given rise to the question of whether there could be life on the other planets as well. This idea is of course a most obvious one for an intelligent being on one such planet, but it is a question that fails to consider the hierarchical structure of Nature. The better question would be: is there life on a higher or lower level of the hierarchy? Or even—is the principle of life an inherent quality of the entire hierarchical structure?

The solar system includes at least one organismic world. We, naturally, take this for granted, and in our deluded objectivity, see this living world as a freak of an otherwise dead nature!

Fact however is that parts of the solar system are organismic! Our living world is part of the larger system, that may seem dead to our relative position in the hierarchy, but it is really the exclusive source of life as we know it. If this so-called dead system is capable to produce and support organismic life, it cannot as a whole be lifeless! After all, our own bodies are made of so-called inorganic matter, the atoms, which are the same as the atoms of which the solar system is made. Therefore, if a part of a natural system is alive, even if this part is quantitatively insignificant, the whole system has the characteristic of being alive. Even before the Earth knew any of the forms of life that were to evolve later, the solar system had to contain a germ or a design for the exact qualities from which life could spring. The solar system has in fact given birth to all life on Earth entirely from its own resources!

This is, as we shall see, an observation of qualitative consequence, and it is the deeper cause for the two principles of form and light.

5. The atomic level

For I have already at times been a boy and a girl and a bush and a bird and a mute fish in the salty waves.

Everything on this Earth, everything we know, does exclusively exist of atoms. There is really nothing but atoms and emptiness all around us. Still—until recently, the reality of the atom did not exist to the human awareness. Before the microscope a simple outlook on nature did not allow us to become aware of the atom, and so the celestial bodies were the only indication for nature to be organized hierarchically. Now, we realize that there are many tiny boxes in every bigger box, that every piece of matter consists of millions of atoms like small solar systems forming a specific structure. People still haven't seen an atom with their own eyes, which makes the fact of a hierarchical organization in micro space somewhat unreal and hard to visualize.

For a time, the atom was considered the smallest, indivisible unit in Nature. As always, the limitations of the observer were imposed on the object of observation. As always, nature proved the assumption of a final spatial limit wrong.

As early as 1898, the American geologist Thomas Chrowder Chamberlin was speculating that atoms were complex organizations and seats of enormous energies. That there was an internal structure to the atom that could be intimated from several lines of research, among them the study of radioactivity. For atoms to emit particles, as they were found to do in the laboratories of Becquerel and the Curies, and for these emissions to change them from one element to another, atoms had to be more than simple, indivisible units that their name (from the Greek for 'cannot be cut') implied. Atomic physics had finally identified three principal constituents of the atom by 1932—the proton, the neutron and the electron. The existence of the atomic nucleus as discovered by Rutherford in 1911 led finally to the exploration of the electron that Niels Bohr found to inhabit discrete orbits, or shells surrounding the nucleus.

For a time, Bohr thought of the atom as a miniature solar system. Despite the striking similarities, this comparison came to a halt, when Newtonian mechanics didn't work with the atom. The number of electrons in a given atom is determined by the electrical charge of the nucleus, which is the key to the atoms identity. Since the electrical charge of the nucleus and the gravitational force of a star cannot yet be interrelated by mathematics, it was necessary to introduce quantum mechanics to replace Newtonian mechanics—and the atom was no longer a miniature solar system!

This is one more example of how the most stunning similarities can become ignored for the sake of a little unexplained difference, even if this difference may only be one of perspective and of spatial and temporal hierarchy. While to mathematical systems, this difference may seem essential, to the observer of natural design and of evolutionary change it is still the sameness in principle that can provide the most valid insights.

The question we have to ask is—why does the solar system take the same basic form as the atomic system? To those, who explain the solar system with gravity as the initial cause this question cannot be answered, since gravity is, as we know, not the force responsible for the atomic structure. But is quantum mechanics really so essentially different form Newtonian mechanics? Let us consider an electron that falls from an outer orbit to an inner orbit, emitting a photon. Energy loss makes the electron move into a closer orbit. The same thing happens to a planet if it loses mass. The reason, why Jupiter moves in an outer orbit relative to the Earth is its greater mass. If we could take energy (mass) away from it, its orbit would also change into a closer one.

While on the higher hierarchical level a planet would take up its new orbit gradually, an electron is supposedly jumping into its new orbit instantaneously. Apart from the fact, that we know practically nothing about this idea of an instantaneous quantum jump, we have to expect these vast differences in speed, if comparing a system on separate scales of the hierarchy.

A phenomenon compared on different levels of the hierarchy will, relative to an observer from a particular level, always show apparent differences in mechanics. Quantum mechanics and Newtonian mechanics describe the same basic design on two separate levels of the hierarchy. In order to replace the two unrelated systems by a unified mechanics of all nature, the differences in mechanics must be understood in terms of scale and of evolutionary 'time.' At the time when the universe was still young, and the stars did not yet exist, there was no Newtonian mechanics, only quantum mechanical processes which accounted for all phenomena in existence. At this time, which marks the beginning of gravitational evolution, the various levels of hierarchical scale as we know them now did not yet exist. Only the universal expansion, which equals the speed of gravitational evolution, led to a distinction between the generation of the quantum process—and Newtonian processes—which therefore have to be defined as quantum process plus expansion.

Also, the energy that powers a proton and the energy that powers the sun are quite identical.

It is actually exclusively the energy of the atomic particles which powers the sun! The sun is but an aggregation of nucleus particles, which means, that we are not comparing two separate systems at all, but rather two quantities of the same unit which is the atomic particle. The sun's heat is the energy released from the particles that already contain the needed energy from all beginning.

Moreover, the sun is not just an aggregation of atoms and the sum of their released energies, but it also contains all other atomic properties and even takes on the form of the atomic system.

One of these atomic properties is the light produced in the sun.

As we have seen, it is the form of the atom that determines the light frequencies of the sun. It is really the atom, which is shining down on the Earth, and which brings forth life by releasing its energy! The sun is but a word for a sum of atoms, or for a higher evolutionary level of the atom in its evolution towards the final levels of its reality in time.

Also, the gravitational force of the sun is a function of the sum of the atomic weight of the atomic building-blocks, which make up the sun's mass.

However, there seems to be a major contradiction to this simple quantitative approach: The nucleus of the atom is held together by a force much greater than the gravitation that stabilizes the form of the sun! While gravitation has a relative strength of 1, the strong force has a relative strength of 10^{41}

Also—the range of the Strong Force is only $<3x10^5$, whereas the range of gravity is thought to be infinite.

This vast difference in range and strength seems to mock the idea that the sun is the sum of all the properties of the atom. This is, if the hierarchical movement of the atomic evolution is left out of consideration!

Space, argued Mach, is not a thing, but an expression of interrelationships among events. 'All masses and all velocities and consequently all forces are relative,' he wrote. In fact, the gravitational field has only a relative existence. Relative to large objects, gravity does a fine job at holding them together, but on the atomic level, where the universal expansion of space cannot create a gravitational potential, gravitation fails to do the required job of creating and maintaining the spherical and rotating form. Gravitation is, during the expansion of the universe, gradually evolving to reach its final strength, where in microcosmic space it is still too weak to make a difference. So where does the Strong Force come from—a force that is a contracting force as is gravity?

Einstein provides the clue for this, when showing that the force of gravitation is dependent on the geometry of space:

'Matter, (consisting of dense particles), curves space, and what we call gravitation is but the acceleration of objects as they slide down the toboggan runs described by their trajectories in time, through the undulations of space.'

Gravitation is dependent on mass (amount of atoms) and on the existence of space. Since both did not exist before the universe started to expand, gravity has to be considered a product of the universal expansion, which is also evolutionary time for the atom. The strong force however had to exist even in the beginning, in order for particles to exist and have form! The strong force is hence the only aspect of the Contracting Force before expansion—while gravity is an evolutionary product of expansion, and determined by mass, which is the amount and the weight of atoms participating in the field.

As I will demonstrate in the chapter on dualities, gravitation is but a new, evolving generation of the strong force, and is growing until it equals the strong force again—as it has at the beginning of the universe! In principle, there is only one Contracting Force of which the strong force and gravitation are polar aspects with opposite direction if regarded in a linear way. In reality, the contracting force moves through the Hierarchy in a kind of implosion right down to the atomic nucleus, while the expanding force slowly evolves the form of the universe as a whole.

Whenever a cycle is completed, and a new repetition of form is created, the contracting force and the expanding force will both change direction and act towards their opposite pole. This means, that the gravitational potential of the fully expanded universe is translated into the design of its composite building blocks, before it disintegrates. This is how the strong force, all this amazing energy, entered the atom in the first place, and this is why the first particle knew how exactly to start a new evolutionary cycle.

Since particles are far older than the sun, we find them to be very stable systems today. It takes a long time to find this stability. The stars, on the other hand are still in their process of finding a stable structure. It is known that stars, in their process of burning out their fuel and producing very high temperatures, will collapse eventually into smaller sizes. A highly evolved star sorts itself into layers, like an onion, its gaseous core surrounded by concentric shells. Eventually its iron core grows until the star collapses and crystallizes into a steely sphere, a neutron star.

This neutron star spins rapidly on its axis and resembles nothing as much as a giant atomic nucleus.

In this stage of its evolution, a star is very comparable indeed to the nucleus of an atom, if the relative positions in space and time are taken into account. It would seem that the evolution of stars includes the various stages of collapse and progress until the star has reached the size of an atomic nucleus once again! The evolution of stars serves then as a new generation of their basic building blocks, and is driven by the hierarchical cycles programmed into the simplicity of the atom.

The spatial hierarchy can also be viewed as a hierarchy of temporal continuity, where the smaller building blocks of which the larger ones are made, are also the older, mature generation. All forms, that have arisen from the atomic evolution, like the solar system for example, are then but stages of the atomic evolution, where the atom contains the blue print for all the higher hierarchical structures.

The differences between Relativity and quantum physics can then not be differences in principle, but are rather created by the observer looking at a cycle in a linear way from the inside, when comparing two stages of space/time evolution.

Newtonian mechanics breaks down in quantum space only because it does not take into account the last universe, and the directions of the evolutionary processes of matter in terms of the hierarchical (fractal) reproduction of form.

It is utterly impossible to describe the workings of the universe by looking at isolated systems and their particular mechanics! The universe can only be understood if our constants and laws are seen as relative to the evolution of the final form. Just as we understand our immediate surroundings in terms of form and reproductive movements, the universe can be understood in exactly the same way. Quantity is never a factor which we should emphasize on when trying to discern the design of a system, especially not the vastness of the universe. It is really only an indicator, from which scale in space and time we are observing a any system from the inside.

The differences of the laws of the solar system, as compared to the atom, are but a consequence of expansion (= level of evolution), which is usually expressed as space and time—and that holds true throughout the hierarchy. This has so far not been discovered by mathematics, since the scale factor of the Hierarchy is not simply quantitative, but connected to certain polarities, where form evolves and disintegrates, and where matter follows the evolution of form rather than the mechanics of primordial physical forces.

All the laws we discover in the universe today, were already numerically implicit in the design of the first particles, which still make up everything the universe is.

This is why the solar system reminds us of the atomic system, and it may be that we are supposed to see this intrinsic sameness, so that we may discover the master plan, the stunning simplicity of the One a midst the diversity of all its manifestations.

The assumption of modern physics that the forces, particularly gravitation, are responsible for the sameness between the cosmic Systems is not incorrect, but it explains nothing. Of course, it is gravity which creates the spherical shape of a star and its planets, but since gravity is a consequence of matter, it must be matter, or the basic design of the nucleus, which knows in the first place about how to achieve the spherical form. The Forces are the medium which the atomic nucleus employs. Gravitation is no more cause for the spherical form than sunlight is causal for a seed to grow into an oak tree.

No matter how impressive the sun is, and how different its system appears due to its temporal stage in evolution—it is still but a manifestation of the inherent qualities of the atom, and a stage of the atomic evolution towards a higher level.

If we understand this, we can deduce the most essential quality of the atom—it contains the blueprint of life and possibly of all its living forms!

If a solar system can produce life without outside assistance, and if this solar system consists entirely of atoms, and if it also mimics the shape and the behaviour of the atom—then the ability to create life must be an inherent quality of the atom! The sun releases light and evolves life, but it is the atom that contains the light of the stars, and that carries the seed of life.

Organic life cannot be created by random chemical brews over time. The atom contains the principle of organic life, just like a seed or a gene. It is a true fractal.

To speak of inorganic matter at all is then, since all matter consists of atoms, categorically nonsensical in a fractal universe.

So—how many civilizations may exist then, inside the body of any observer? Nature is of course nowhere infinite, as infinity would mean infinitely small worlds within the atom as well as infinitely large levels of reality. Certainly, there can be no carbon or water as we know it on these microscopic worlds to sustain life as we know it, but there could still be life, similar to ours even, on a smaller scale. Fact is that a proton is a world much like any planet of our own scale—it has celestial companions, some electron rises and sets in the darkness of space, and it is part of huge galaxies of molecules—and it has a surface! What does the surface of a proton or an even smaller world actually look like? Smooth and polished, as in an academic textbook? Or rugged, mountainous maybe? Or has it patterns instead of no texture at all? Any speculation about the reality on such worlds naturally sound like science fiction because we are not used to visualizing reality on the microscopic scales. Nevertheless, the microscopic and the sub-microscopic worlds have to possess some kind of surface; they definitely do have day and night—and if we could only see their reality close enough (if we were small enough), we would discern something. Possibly we would find vegetation growing from the frequencies of light emitted by the electrons or other particles—on a 'soil' made up of matter on such a small scale that it appears to us as pure energy—because of its faster time-table.

Possibly, we could find life-forms, or see artificial structures, if we could walk on such a quasi-planetary surface. This cannot be excluded based on the pressures of the strong force, because we know and perceive only our own small fragment of the natural spectrum—and a continuity of the hierarchy in both directions, as well as a consistency in design would make it highly probable.

Is it likely that life-forms inhabit the galaxies of the inner worlds? Our own bodies may then be the home to billions of civilizations, living on a much faster time scale for only seconds of our time and all of them unaware, that the clusters of galaxies around them are really part of an even larger organic level of the hierarchical order—the human body. The suggestion that the human body is host to very small organisms of subatomic scale is also suggested by the fact that even on the observable scale the human body is known to host more micro-organisms than there are people on Earth!

In the context of what we already know about the hierarchical continuity in both directions relative to our position, it is, apart from psychological limitations, more speculative to assume a sudden end to this continuity, than it is to expect it to continue following the observable patterns implicit in the natural numbers. Our range of vision must however not limit our ability to include infinity as a possible quality of nature (or of a looping spiral).

The very existence of a hierarchy which has been extended ever since the sun gave us the first hint of something larger, is reason enough to assume that Nature could go smaller that the quark and larger than this universe. There could be a beyond.

What clues does the universe give, and what does logic suggest, if nature does nothing but repeat its basic patterns on all the various known levels of the hierarchy? Will it not repeat ALL of its basic levels of organization? If it repeats the hierarchical spheres and vortices—will the universe not also repeat its living forms, including the human form somewhere in its microcosmic depth, just as the spherical form of the solar- system is repeated on the atomic scale? The natural principles of simple mechanics don't just appear and disappear, or cease to apply beyond our range of vision! They actually have to be consistent, cyclical, hierarchical and continuous in order to maintain their existence. There is no room for randomness! To find out why organisms are part of the universal structure, we will need to explore the more remote levels of the hierarchy, where structures become difficult for us to discern. Let us therefore change direction and contemplate the higher levels of macro-cosmic reality—the galaxies and clusters of stars.

6. The level of the galaxies and clusters

The Milky Way system includes roughly a hundred billion stars and its radius reaches through more than $3x10^4$ light years. Seventy-five percent of those stars do interestingly have one or more companions with which they dance as they go down their galactic track. Of all the strange multiple stars disclosed by the telescope and spectroscope only the simple double stars reveal their masses. This is because the tempos and patterns of 'three-star tangos, four-star fandangos and many-star mazurkas' are often too complicated even for modern mathematics.

Interestingly, it has been discovered that the Milky Way is a huge rotating disk, more precisely a spiraling disk. Many galaxies are called spiral galaxies because they have a disk-like form and are rotating. These rotating spirals are each a system of stars similar to the Milky Way System.

Still larger cosmic systems are clusters of galaxies: Each cluster is made up of many galaxies, the larger ones having thousands of constituents. These clusters have rather symmetrical shapes, indicating rotation. The scale of a cluster of galaxies is about $2x10^7$ light years.

The hierarchical level of the galaxies is again a sum of all the smaller level-solar systems, and therefore a further evolutionary step of the atom on its journey through the hierarchy. A galaxy is essentially behaving like a solar system since it is nothing but a quantity of solar systems. It also behaves like an atom, since it is nothing but a quantity of atoms. There are only those hierarchical variations where the atom, during its evolution, releases its evolutionary potential in hierarchical stages. This gives the impression of asymmetry between the atom and the galactic systems.

The clusters are also a repetition of the basic form and of the qualities of the atom on an even higher scale and they are also a stage of the hierarchical evolution of the spherical form.

Just like the atom has a core—the nucleus—the galaxies and clusters also have a dense core, which can be attributed to gravitation or, if we want to make a little more sense of it, to the form of the atom, which employs gravitation to reproduce itself on higher levels.

The Milky Way contains, we must not forget, what we define as organic life, and it has, from its own resources alone, produced the human form! The same can be said for the cluster of which the Milky Way is a part, without weakening the argument by these considerations of quantity and size. The simplicity of this fact should not distract of its undeniable reality or from its utmost relevance to physics and biology! Nature, on the macro-cosmic scale, does not introduce any new principles in addition to its basic design, but projects the atomic design onto a larger canvas provided by expansion.

The known hierarchical levels of macro-cosmic space provide the form of the universe with a structural framework, and the atom with a continuous field for projection. The continuity of nature in both directions of the hierarchy is given by a polarity that projects the large, finalized form back onto its microcosmic starting point by contraction and by disintegration.

The atomic design has thus the characteristics of a 'perpedo mobile,' where the energy lost by expansion/evolution returns as contraction and is further recycled by a disintegration of form. Nature thus does not need any additional forces or influential factors beside the atomic form, as it is in the nature of the atom to achieve the necessary simplicity capable of perpetuating itself as what we call creation.

We may ask whether the continuity of nature exceeds the boundaries of the known universe, or whether the hierarchical ladder has any end at all. As far as the form of this universe is concerned, its evolutionary range reaches only from the atomic nucleus to the size of the expanded universe—from where it contracts back to the size of the nucleus—to generate a new reincarnation of universe.

But let us dive back into the realms of micro-space, to look at what science considers being the very smallest building-blocks of nature. Are quarks the beginning of all physical evolution and the very bottom end of the hierarchical ladder?

7. The subatomic and quark level

Every atomic particle is a box which contains even smaller boxes, which are called quarks. Quarks are the basic units of any manifestation of matter in the known universe. In the beginning, the cosmos was an ocean of free quarks, and

other elementary particles. For every 10^6 anti-quarks, so says

cosmology, there were $10^6 + 1$ quarks, so that only a few quarks survived the annihilation between antimatter and matter.

Science assigns three 'colors' to quarks: red, green and blue, to account for three types of behaviour in quarks. Each coloured quark can have one of six different 'flavors': up, down, strange, charm, bottom and top. Hence, there are altogether 3x6 = 18 different sorts of quarks, and of course, each quark has its own anti-quark.

The eighteen quarks and six leptons are the basic elements that make up all matter in this universe. Of course, we should be careful with such statements since so far they have always proven wrong, and even smaller material building blocks have constantly emerged when we thought it impossible. Still, we discover hundreds of new particles where before, we thought there were definitely only the proton, the neutron, and the electron. Recently, we discovered that subatomic particles shot into each other at high velocities, break up into a spectrum of even smaller 'possibilities', that might create just about anything! The essence of quantum mechanics is that everything possible can happen at this quantum level. But not everything does happen, of course. This is the where observation and creation meet!

Who knows, what those physicists shooting subatomic particles into each other will create? New universes in the microcosm? Creation itself—whatever it might be—seems to act from the probability structures of the subatomic worlds, and whatever the scientists do to those worlds, changes everything about their reality. But also vice versa—those small worlds influence and determine us humans on a medical, biological, emotional, and even cerebral level!

Subatomic particles are mathematically found to be very interesting, as they follow intricate patterns of weak and electromagnetic interactions that appear like a weave of magical numbers, as if they carried the original design or formula, that has created and creates all of our material, emotional and intellectual reality!

It could be the quark level at the bottom end of the hierarchy, where nothing smaller exists. Quarks and subatomic particles definitely define the boundary between what to us is material, and what we see as energy-waves. As thoughts...

Quarks have been found to have practically no mass, though their anatomy has been probed on scales

down to some 10-18 meters. However, a nucleon which consists of quarks, does have mass. To be even more simple: the smallest manifestation of actual matter consists of nothing but energy, the location of which cannot even be determined, and not of smaller pieces of solid matter that could contribute to the mass of the whole nucleus!

It is well known from $E=mc^2$ that energy and matter are

reversible expressions, depending on the speed of light. But it is quite an experience to face that matter, no matter what it is, does not as such exist, as soon as it is looked at in detail! This fact has to be somehow ignored by some mechanistic physicists in order for them to maintain a philosophy of mechanistic materialism without any material basis at the very root of quantum physics.

What we commonly see as solid objects, are in truth but an emptiness of rotating energy without any solidity whatsoever. It cannot be disputed however that the human senses, including our visual sense, do not perceive reality as it really is. When we look at an apple, for example, we don't even see even a tiny fraction of its actual reality! We cannot see the surface, except some play of light from the view of our position. We also can't see its composite parts, the cells and the molecules and atoms. All those rotating electrons are simply too fast, and the spatial scales too remote for our eyes—and the brain could never cope with those box-in-a-box realities, even if the eye could be aware of them.

All we can really see, is light (colour), and shape. The eye sees no detail of structure and is blind towards the hierarchical organization that defines even its own structure, and just as blind to that of anything else. Now, if we could see what reality really is, not only would we then have to be able to detect all those molecules and atoms, but we would mostly see nothing at all—because the apple is entirely made up of near mass-less, non-material quarks, or in other words—pure energy, that moves far too fast for the human eye to follow. What we see, when we look at an apple, is an illusion imposed by the structure of our eye, which can only tell us about the method and the limits of the observer—than it can ever give us a clue on the actual reality of the observed object.

With the event of quantum-mechanics the question if matter, or the particles amounting to matter, are really the solid building-blocks we always thought they were, has become the great philosophical paradox of physics.

Particles, so says quantum physics, are not at all individually observable, but can only be identified in groups and behave according to so-called quantum probabilities. These probabilistic patterns of matter are not random, but they are influenced by observation, more precisely by the mind of the scientist conducting the experiment. What we used to consider only as solid particles, can be described as waves or probability-waves, and this wave-like character is just as real as the particle character of these smallest units of matter.

The wave-particle duality does not proclaim that the existence of matter is unreal, but rather that matter has a solid aspect and a wave-like aspect. Matter, and consequently the universe as a whole, can thus be described in terms of waves, and also in terms of particles.

Philosophically, this discovery has not even started to have its impact, but physically there is no merit in doubting the reality of either aspect of the wave-particle duality. The hierarchical organization of spherical forms, including the particles, is of course not affected by an alternative description as waves—it can be represented in various ways, even as sound.

The idea suggested by 'string theory,' that particles might be string-like rather than spherical, attempts to explain the wave-properties of particles with their actual shape, in order to account for their variant behaviour in mechanistic terms. The strength of string theory is its dualistic structure, where there are always two ends, or sides, to the story of possible interactions. Every one of those theories contributes a perspective that, taken by itself, can be quite correct and even interesting.

But if we want to really know about the reality of our physical universe, we cannot just keep quantifying the manifestations we recognize with our senses and with visual aids, but have to decipher the design conveyed by the quark, its wave nature— and its ability to receive frequencies which may hold the answer to where quarks are getting their information!

Lao-Tzu defined the first cause of the All as the 'Tao' that cannot be explained or understood. He saw the physical universe as an illusion.

Matter has, so it seems, no independent existence beside energy, and could easily be an illusion created by the material observer from a slower time-scale, observing (and creating) phenomena on much faster time-scales.

If other senses, like the sense of touch, seem to confirm our visual experience, this is due to the same hierarchical remoteness from the structural detail of the fast-moving object. In truth, we can never touch anything at all, since electrons repel each other. All we can do is to 'fall down the curves of their spatial structure' as Einstein has put it. If electrons, both of the hand and of the object we 'touch,' didn't repel each other, or in other words, if the spherical form didn't protect its integrity by rotation, we would feel nothing at all. We could then actually walk right through a wall!

If we consider that quarks are pure energy, it appears plausible, that they demarcate indeed the smallest unit of all reality. However, if energy and matter are only distinguishable in terms of speed, it could be that the quark, if observed from a very small and fast position in the hierarchy, say from the atomic level, will have all the characteristics of a material building block. Then, the quark could still be a box containing smaller boxes that can only be detected if observed from a lower hierarchical level from where they might appear dense and slow enough to qualify as matter to that micro-observer. Matter could then not be defined by us as something that has mass. Matter and mass are then merely subjective experiences of an observer, observing a substance from his own position in space, and from his own speed.

If a substance is too remote, relative to our hierarchical position, for us to detect its small size or its position, it is experienced as energy. To assume the quark to be the definitely smallest unit of matter would then be in contradiction with the relativity between matter and energy that could allow for even smaller units on a 'material' plane. We must probably admit that any differentiation between matter and energy is purely subjective, and will depend entirely on the size or scale of the observer.

On the other hand, the form of the physical universe we know must have a material polarity, the bottom end of which is the atomic nucleus. The quark therefore marks, relative to the polarity field of the universe, the beginning of material existence and development. It may be that we will never detect anything smaller than the quark or larger than the universe, even with our aided senses, because the form of this universe is all we might possibly become aware of. What we call the physical universe summarizes the form of which we are a part, and everything more remote could be too fast or too slow for us to qualify as physical, if viewed from our hierarchical scale and from within the universal form.

If the particles are the smallest massive units of the universe, one should ask what the function of the quark may be in regard to the evolution of the physical universe. The answer to this can only be found in the mechanics of form! When a tree reproduces its form, the finalized form will pass itself down to the level of the seed, which then contains the design of the future form. The seed must be compared with the atomic nucleus, since it is the starting point and design of the tree's life cycle; the point from where the expansion/evolution of the new form starts. But how does the tree-form descend the hierarchical ladder to arrive at the seed level as complete as it was before? There has to be a projecting factor capable of transporting form into micro-space. This task is achieved by the genes of the tree, which carry the final form down into the seed. Every natural form reproduces itself in this way! First there is expansion/growth, where the seed or the egg-cell moves up the hierarchical ladder of evolution, and the second half of the life-cycle is the projection of the final form back into micro-space, which is the exact opposite of expansion. After this descent of form, it eventually disintegrates, and the physical matter assembled by the form also descends into micro-space and also awaits a new life-cycle.

The descent from the hierarchically larger space can be identified as contraction, which is a projection onto the point of minimum expansion, while preserving the original form.

The quark, or a subatomic particle, is relative to the form of the universe like the biological gene, which passes down the form of the previous generation to the new generation. It contains the forms which evolution will eventually finalize and it gives the nucleon the complete design for the evolution of a new universe. This logic will sound surprising, but is, as we will notice, not only consistent but quite unavoidable in the context of form.

Since the 'genetic code' of the universal form is passed down the hierarchy of spatial expansion, it must physically be called a contraction. The quark thus conveys the contraction potential of the fully expanded universe, which is the strong force! The direction of the strong force is for this reason reversed as compared to gravitation.

If the three quarks of a particle are pulled apart, the strong force actually becomes stronger the more distant the quarks become from one another. Planets, on the other hand, if pulled into a more distant orbit from the sun, will feel the gravitational pull of the sun less, the further they are moved away from it.

This shows that the direction and the strength of the strong force are derived from the maximum point of the universal expansion.

When we say, the universe passes down its 'genetic code' onto its minimum by contraction, no collapsing of the universe following its expansion is meant. The contraction is happening simultaneously with expansion, as far as the gravitational potential and the passing down of form is concerned. The universe is eventually going to disintegrate—but what is passed down to the nucleon via quark is only the design, the expansion potential, and not the mass of the old universe.

Even 'genetic' potential is only passed down as far as it is needed. Therefore, and to exclude all unneeded quantum possibilities, quarks and the anti-quarks, representing the genetic code, had to annihilate each other in the beginning of the universe, so that only one quark out of every 106 quarks survived this 'selective process.' The surviving quarks then represent the 'genetic' information required by the young universe.

The quark level, by virtue of its wave nature, has to contain the key to all forms, to all phenomena contained in this universe. Also, the existence of life has to be included in the design projected into the quark.

Life forms are not only made of nothing but quarks physically, but they are made of quark-properties as well. The quark has to therefore be as latently complex and as intrinsically organic as any life-form it constitutes.

All the information needed to form genes, chromosomes, human beings and the entire universe has to be part of the magical weave that is the quark-design. If organic and inorganic matter alike are made of the same quarks—there can be no substantial difference between organic and inorganic matter—and every form we know, has to be intimately related to every other form.

Hence, the quark can be seen as a condensed mirror image of all forms contained in the universe, which is explained only by the numerological simplicity of its design and by the harmonic patterns it receives from the maximum levels of universal form. Microcosm and Macrocosm have after all symmetrical harmonics, despite of the hierarchical differences created by the factor of expansion/evolution.

The secret of what the quark really is can almost not be told in words. The entire secret is in the number three! Creation proceeds in steps one-two-three...Oneness becomes two by division, by direction, by polarity. Step three is about reproduction, about appearance of form. It is about the 'Holy Trinity' that makes up all things.

Lao Tzu says the Three created the 'ten thousand things.' That is all the quark is—the Three, that is the exact mathematical formula with the function to make up a new One!

Geometrically, the one is a circle or a point (small circle); the two is a straight line connecting two points. The third step of evolution—a third point anywhere in the landscape creates a triangle—which is a new dimension, a new One in the second dimension! A new point outside this triangle creates the first form of the third dimension—a tetrahedron or pyramid. This is how Creation works mathematically.

The three quarks making up every atom need but be three. Father, Mother, Son—the trinity that has created a new One!

The essence of life does not, as Darwin thought, suddenly appear from nowhere by random evolution, but is contained and always has been contained in every basic building block of this universe! Evolution has no absolute beginning and no absolute end, but is for this universe defined by the life-cycle of the universal form in the phase of expansion. The evolution of the universe follows the design projected into the quark, which can therefore be identified as the receptor of contraction/reproduction of the universal form at the bottom of matter.

Suspecting what exact role the quark plays at the bottom of the hierarchy of universal form, we will now ask what form the universe takes at its point of maximum expansion!

Does the spherical form continue infinitely, or only to the size of the fully expanded universe? Is the universal form the sole exception to the rule—or does all form reproduce itself hierarchically, because this is the only way form can perpetuate itself?

A deeper look into macro-cosmic reality brings us to the largest observable scale in the universe—the hierarchical level of the super-cluster.

8. The hierarchical level of the super-cluster

When we go to the scale of 2×10^8 light years we come to the scale of the super-clusters. A super-cluster is made up of many clusters. Their shape is however very different from those of smaller-scale systems! The sun, the Milky Way, galaxies and clusters, are all isolated systems in space—that is matter is concentrated in the central region, surrounded by empty space. In contrast, super-clusters are not clearly demarcated; rather, the distribution of matter is net-like, and the empty space is now isolated in holes or 'voids!' Also—super-clusters do not have symmetrical shapes, and show no clear evidence of rotation. How can this peculiarity be explained?

According to Laplace's nebular theory it has to do with the collapsing time of the original gas cloud that will later form the galaxy or the super-cluster. As long as the original gas cloud has a certain amount of angular momentum, then according to Laplace, no matter what its original shape, the body formed after the collapse must have a symmetrical shape indicating rotation. The point is that it takes the gas cloud a certain time to collapse. This time is called the contraction time or the collapsing time. Smaller scale objects have symmetrical forms because they have already completed the contraction process, whereas super-clusters do allegedly not have symmetrical forms because since they require so long a collapsing time, they have, up to now, not yet completed the collapsing process.

This theory of Laplace would mean that the hierarchical continuity of the sphere extends indeed throughout macro-space, and that only the time factor gives the illusion of a discontinuity.

However, there is another, more consistent interpretation to the shape of super-clusters. Granted, that the rotating disk is the ever-perpetuating principle throughout nature, there are still hierarchical levels that deviate from this principle! These levels are the so-called organic levels of the organic molecules, the cells, the organisms, which appear in between the hierarchical levels of the rotating disks.

It may be that not only all the forms we know, like the form of an oak-tree or the human form, constitute a complete system of hierarchical spheres, but that the spherical systems of macrocosm similarly constitute such a complete universal form! Like the human body, which is made of spheres within spheres that find their limit where the complete final form emerges on the organismic level—also the spherical systems on our macro-cosmic scale could continue until they finalize the universal form!

The net-like distribution of matter is hard to explain in terms of a collapsing gas cloud. It is more likely that this particular arrangement of matter in super-clusters, and also their shape, are signs of a patterned structural alignment.

If nature can be said to follow a very basic and simple design, or to obey its own laws as far as the rotating disks are concerned, the total lack of consistency would surprise, if the design for organic life appeared only once or on one level of the hierarchy without being continued on other levels!

A law of nature that creates the spherical form by repeating it hierarchically, must apply to the organic life-forms as well, since the basic parts of the 'organic' levels and of the 'inorganic' levels are on their atomic level identical.

The hierarchical organization of nature as a box in a box system is not explained by science, and unexplainable in principle by the known forces of physics. It rather constitutes the key to a unified understanding of nature, and it demonstrates the paramount position of form, which it serves to organize.

It is the hierarchy itself that closes the cycles of all the natural forms, of all the complex forces involved, and thereby of the only possible understanding of creation as a oneness. If everything is related within the universal hierarchical cycle, there can be no freak appearance of human life, because it would not relate to the hierarchical function of the whole. Nature has to repeat the organic forms we know from our level on some higher level of the hierarchy in order for them to even exist! The net-like distribution of matter in super-clusters and their non-spherical shape indicates a level of organic organization, similar to organic tissue, which is also made up by clusters of supposedly 'dead' or 'inorganic' spheres.

If form generally is organized hierarchically, and repeats itself like the spheres within larger spheres, it would seem impossible that the organic forms in the universe break away from this rule and should exist solely on the planetary level of the Hierarchy. A sole, isolated existence does not connect up with the wider reality enough for it to be created.

In order to understand the nature of the universe, we therefore have to explore the nature of form and its continuity within the hierarchy. If the many forms and phenomena are interconnected and purposeful, their hierarchical patterns in space should be indicative of a deeper reality beyond the complexity of the many, and lead us to the larger box, of which every-thing else, including the super-clusters, is a part.

9. The Principle of Opposite Truths

There is one thing that all forces of nature, all movement, and all form have in common—they can ultimately be understood as dualities of opposites. The ancient Chinese have known this for millennia and called the two forces of the universe—yin and yang.

'The Tao created the One, the One created the Two, the Two created the Three and the Three created all things' —this is how Lao-Tzu saw creation.

As we have seen, all things materialize from the level of the quark, which creates matter always in groups of three quarks per basic unit. It is this number three that the quark symbolizes, which 'makes' all things material. The logical next step towards a unified and comprehensive description of nature is to discern the nature of duality, which according to Lao-Tzu arose directly from the oneness of creation—and which is thus the step before realizing this Oneness itself.

Modern science deals with the concept of the Two only from within a dialectic logic of cause/effect, without exploring the principle itself as relating to Oneness. Naturally, a linear logic can only follow the dualistic pattern of thought blindly, without ever realizing its purpose or its ascent from the original pinpoint of oneness. As a consequence, duality is regularly seen as an antagonistic polarity of either/or—rather than as the two sides to the same coin. This is why the following statement of Niels Bohr can be appreciated as a major contribution to the evolution of non-linear logic. 'A great truth is a truth whose opposite is also a great truth.'

Such statements of great men are generally not heeded as much as their mathematical formulae, because they are supposed to be purely philosophical and of no practical use. For this reason, a unified perception of nature as One has up to now proven well beyond the grasp of the scientific method.

Cosmology has reached a point where the limited frame-work of a conventional scientific method does no longer suffice to relate physical science to universal subjects like the nature and the origin of the universe. So we must learn to trust our deeper human senses, that are so intimately interwoven with the quantum mechanical fabric of the surrounding cosmos to intuitively grasp the simple truth of a design we face every moment of our lives. We have to time our thinking to the movements of nature, and we have to evolve our logic from a linear cause/effect of A to B—logic to a cyclical contemplation of causation that can comprehend cause/effect as reversible poles of the same cyclical phenomenon. Only a logical system that is in accord with the cyclical logic of nature herself can describe nature in a comprehensive way.

For those sceptical of philosophical insight, especially Eastern wisdom, let us contemplate another of Bohr's home-truths—'what seems like a wise word in matters of philosophy, can actually be the solution to some of the most intricate cosmological and human problems if seen in its literal wording. It could hint at a law of nature in a far deeper sense than is gravity or electromagnetism!'

These words should be the daily bread of every scientist interested in discovering the truth.

If related to his great truth whose opposite must also be true, Bohr's statement might just help to reveal the most fundamental law of nature that will explain all other laws!

After we gain insight into this opposite-principle, we next have to establish a clear definition of what an 'opposite' exactly is. The axis on which we have to build the symmetry of equal opposites must be one of movement or change. Therefore, the opposite of a state is the state after a complete transformation! Expansion is the opposite of contraction; hot is the opposite of cold; up is the opposite of down; left is the opposite of right, and outside is the opposite of inside. If Bohr was right, none of these concepts can exist without their opposite. If it is true, that an object is cold, there must be the potential, a time or place of it being hot, and so on. It is not possible to call something small, if there is not the known reference point of big. Left can only exist if there is a right, and if it is true that there is a past, there must also be a future.

Could it be that this rule applies to every single natural phenomenon in existence?

Can there be the concept of a good God, without a bad devil? Can there be a birth without death? Would we see the light, if there were no darkness?

Nature does in fact not even produce a single particle without creating its exact opposite—on sometimes several axis of symmetry! If we look close enough however, we find that nature does not simply create dualistic pairs of opposites that co-exist at the same time.

An object is either left or right, hot or cold, only in relation to the observer or to any other object. But if something is very hot, relative to its surroundings, it will start to cool down, just like a movement to the left will, on a spherical surface (which is all there is), eventually appear on the right of its reference point. So does each thing carry the germ of its opposite, even if the opposite is only a tendency, a potential—or a microcosmic germ...

The opposite principle becomes interesting, when applied to form, say to the form of a tree. What is the opposite of a tree? An anti-matter tree? At this point we have to orientate ourselves on the axis of movement which is the growth of the tree. And we must not be fooled by the preconception that opposites have to necessarily be quantitatively equal. An opposite of light and heavy can never be quantitatively equal to its partner.

The growth of a tree is a movement from small to big, and the pair of opposites can only be the minimum and the maximum points of growth, which are the seed and the mature tree. So it is with all form in Nature!

What is preserved by both opposites is not quantity, but quality (design), which is the complete characteristics of the form. The seed contains the precise blueprint for the mature tree, and the mature tree carries the design for the seed. We all know that trees grow from seed, but it must be realized, that form generally moves within a predetermined cycle of opposite poles. The cycle consisting of expansion/growth and contraction/reproduction is such a duality that preserves the perfect symmetry of form. During the transformation this symmetry appears broken, but when the cycle is complete, it is restored perfectly, and the form can thus be continuous.

If we take a cyclic duality, like birth and death, the connection of opposites is just as clear. At birth we are starting to move towards death, because a beginning without end is impossible. Birth and death are not antagonists, but the two opposites necessary to allow for a cycle of life.

There is the growing physical organization on one side, and physical disintegration on the other. First, form assembles the minerals from the Earth into living matter, and then the same matter breaks up into its constituent minerals through decay.

The pairs of opposites as given by the continuity of form can be reduced to the single duality of growth towards the final form and the disintegration of form back into its basic building blocks.

The duality principle can therefore explain all forces participating in expansion or contraction—in terms of form.

The system (the form) of the universe can thus account for the physical forces if they are seen in their actual functions of expansion and contraction!

In a consistent and connected, fractal nature, the form of the universe must follow the same rules as all other forms. Indeed, the universal expansion, its structural make-up, and the similarities between macrocosm and microcosm guarantee that the universal form moves from a point of minimum expansion to a point of maximum expansion—just like any other natural form. The opposite principle can thus predict developments of universal change, and shed new light on our cause/effect logic as far as the original act of creation of this universe is concerned. Systematically applied, it is the most valuable tool for the discovery of unknown forces in nature.

For example, the existence of the proton could have been predicted by simply turning the known characteristics of the electron to their exact opposite. Knowing the electron has negative charge and is found in orbit around another object, and that it has little mass—the duality principle would have described the proton as being positively charged, massive and centred. This is, in principle, how the opposite principle can be put to work.

Following this example, we can practically discover anything, if we already know one half of its symmetrical manifestation or any motion or change relating to it.

It also becomes possible to test the truth of a theory, by using the principle in its reverse function—only if the opposite of a dualistic fact is true, the fact itself is true!

Example: The sun rises in the morning. Rising is part of a duality (rise - descend). So, the sun has to descend in the evening—which is true.

Example: Form produces light. (We know, that light is a consequence of the atomic structure). And light also produces form! This is true, as the sun-light is needed for the evolution of all known planetary forms to occur.

Example: The universe expands. This is only true, if it also contracts. Since contraction is actually happening to all forms throughout the universe, the theory of expansion is correct.

If we now apply the opposite principle to the unknown, we receive some interesting results:

Example: If all existence is infinite on the large scale, it must also be infinite on the microcosmic scale!

Example: If the universe is unlimited, it must also be bounded!

Example: If death terminates life, so must life terminate death!

Example: If the universe is spherical, it must also be hyperbolic!

These results are quite correct, as we will find out. Such examples can be continued indefinitely and without a single exception to the rule. Forms are dualities of opposites, which includes the universal form.

The principle of opposite truths can be tested by every example that may come to mind; it is extremely useful and absolutely reliable. Its total generality is able to precisely account for all change in the universe—in terms of the physical forces and fundamentally—in terms of the duality of form.

10. The principle of mutually attractive opposites

When studying the behaviour of opposite polarities, like that given by the flow of space and time, it seems at first that the dualistic poles have a tendency to diverge infinitely from each other. The universe shows no clear sign of ever stopping to expand, and the great stars contract ever more and collapse to ever smaller sizes. The past becomes more remote, while time expands further into the future. If the movement of time continues forever into the same direction, we are facing infinities on a linear scale, where there can be no boundary—while we know all the rest of nature to be bounded!

However, on the surface of a sphere, two opposite directions starting from any point, will eventually converge and meet up again, reversing their initial direction. This principle, which is immanent in spherical geometry, can be observed throughout nature—since all of nature is spherically organized.

If diverging opposites eventually start to approach each other, following a predetermined cycle, they can be said to attract each other. From the point of maximum distance between the two opposites, they move back towards each other, reversing their identity!

Every form in existence has this predetermined range of expansion, given by its seed or basic building block on one hand—and the final size on the other.

Form moves through time as a wave—oscillating between the point of minimum expansion and the point of maximum expansion. This is the case for absolutely every form in the universe, like stars, trees, animals, humans.

The actual point here is that the minimum and maximum poles of form are qualitatively identical. The seed of a tree contains the exact mirror image of the final tree, and the human genes contain a precise microcosmic copy of the mature human.

Therefore, if symmetry is not always a strictly quantitative parity, the opposite poles of every form have to be considered a perfect symmetry, where both sides of the symmetry are absolutely identical, apart from scale.

Symmetries are usually defined quantitatively, meaning that both halves have to measure the same after a transformation.

This is why the most fundamental symmetry—that of form and its germ—has not been discovered by theoretical physics. Of course, there are various symmetry—and super-symmetry—theories in physics tackling some of the omnipresent quantitative symmetries by elaborate mathematical means, but a profound comprehension of symmetry, as relates to the original Oneness, has not been achieved.

The key to recognizing and understanding symmetries is to know why and for how long they remain 'imperfect,' when the time scale of the observer differs considerably from that of the observed reality!

Symmetries have always been associated with divine perfection, and the 'imperfect' symmetries we find in our universe today are considered to be 'broken.' Science is now trying to detect what cause has led to this 'destruction' of the initial symmetries. Convoluted mathematical models are the only result.

If, however, symmetries are seen in the light of the hierarchical organization of form and in the context of simple duality, the problem of 'broken' symmetries immediately disappears—since any transformation like the expansion of the universe is so slow that humans see only ever an incomplete, seemingly unchanging transformation. The symmetry between quark and universe cannot be perceived when looking at a badger!

Let us further contemplate the thesis that opposite forces actually move towards each other, in other words—are mutually attractive! If a truth is only true where its opposite is also true, we have to deduce a strong connection between opposites that reverse their identities.

We notice that electrons are pulled towards protons, and that warm air cools down while warming up cold air—that things try to become each others opposite. Even cosmology has long discussed the possibility of the expanding universe eventually starting to collapse again, due to, as it is explained, increasing gravitation that may suffice to decelerate the expansion enough for it to stop. Then the universe would start collapsing, until it shrinks back to its original size. So would time, many speculate, have to run backwards, until it ceases to exist...

This machine-like model of the universe is of course in complete contradiction with the behaviour of every-thing it contains, and it fails to comprehend the mechanism of expansion/contraction as we know it from all known scales. It may not seem relevant to pure physics that such a universe would have no purpose—but it is also forever impossible to account for creation and existence by giving it an absolute beginning and an absolute end, or by overlooking life in the context of cosmogony.

The only model of the universe that does not contradict its observable realities, is one that expands and contracts in the same way any other natural form does, and which allows for the same cyclical continuities as are fundamental to all other forms.

This would indeed mean that the expanding universe will eventually collapse, but it does not happen the mechanical way as physics predicts! A tree that has grown from its seed, will not eventually reverse its direction and start shrinking again, until it reaches the size of a seed. It will instead produce new seeds and then, much later, disintegrate. Even a star, which is only a building block of universal form, does not simply shrink back in a reversal of its initial growth. It produces new 'seeds' like atomic nuclei and light, and it can disintegrate in many ways. The shrinking of a star may not apply equally to all forms above our scale, but even a star does have no absolute beginning or an absolute end. It oscillates from expansion to contraction and back, as all forms do.

A star, after it has accumulated enough mass through its gravity, will take on a split personality. Its core contracts, as it runs low on fuel, while the outer layers expand and cool. The star becomes a 'red giant.' Ultimately, the stellar atmosphere boils away into space, leaving behind a naked core, a massive dense sphere only about the size of the Earth—a white dwarf star. When the mass is finally too great for the atomic structure to withstand its pressure, the atoms will collapse and the star will further collapse to become a neutron star of very small size. After a time, even the neutrons are not going to keep up with the tremendous pressure and a 'black hole' will be born. The mass is now so great and the pressure so incredible, that the size of the star has shrunk into nothing. Its existence can now only be detected by the terrible strength of its contraction force.

Now, if opposites didn't attract each other, a black hole would keep contracting forever. But what happens at this stage is that a black hole, like any other object under pressure, gathers a huge potential for expansion, and it will eventually reverse its direction and—explode!

It has been discussed, whether a black hole could actually create a whole new universe by means of a fluctuation of this potential. What we must accept as a fact is that there is an inbuilt tendency for any contraction to eventually move towards its opposite—and expand again. Stars make no exception to the principle of mutually attractive opposites. They have a minimum and a maximum, and the fluctuation between the two constitutes their form.

A general law of nature should apply to each and every aspect of existence. Hence, we will leave the boundaries of pure physics for a moment and show with a few examples, how in fact the law of reversing opposites or of 'mutually attractive opposites' determines our life from the behaviour of plants and animals, to psychological, economic, political, and even spiritual conditions.

When the sun rises in the morning, it consistently moves towards its setting in the evening—and vice versa.

From birth we move towards death—and vice versa.

Darkness moves towards light and vice versa.

The last will be the first (bible).

Matter changes into energy—and vice versa.

The higher we rise—the deeper we can fall.

Forbidden fruit taste better.

Rare things rise in value; large supply lowers the price.

The more grass is cut, the denser it grows.

When we hold onto things (or animals, people), we will lose them.

If a culture, sex, religion, or race is suppressed, it will eventually start fighting for liberation and strive towards a reversal of the balance of power.

In order to jump up from the ground, we have to lower ourselves towards it first!

Such obvious and varied examples hint at the universal spectrum of the principle of mutually attractive opposites.

Even the long-lived protons will at some stage become unstable and change into their opposite—electrons (and mesons). On the surface, protons and electrons are opposites that attract each other, without ever really reversing their identity, but their electromagnetic attraction is in reality a signal for the large-scale cycle of attraction that will eventually restore the original symmetry of the atom. Only because of this cyclical identity-change of protons and electrons can the form of the atom exist and continue. The large time-scale of this reversal causes the stability and the relative invariance of electrons and protons. It also causes us to miss observing it.

The wave/particle duality of quantum theory is but a specific study of a universal phenomenon that points directly at the solution to the origin-problem, which can only be answered by duality, and in how duality connects, and leads, to Oneness.

If we now apply the principle of mutually attractive opposites to the open questions of cosmology, we receive some very interesting results:

A system that is finite must move towards the infinite—and every infinite system will move towards the finite (or carry the germ of the finite).

Finite systems like stars appear in numbers that stretch towards the infinite, while form, which is infinite itself, always moves towards its precise, limited and finite manifestation.

Another example is the cyclical nature of 'time': If the past moves towards the future—the future must also move towards the past! This can happen via tachyons that travel backwards in time, or, as many speculate, via the collapse of the universe. That time moves in cycles is a familiar experience on our scale, but the opposite principles predict 'time' itself to be a cycle where the future goes the path of all things, and will eventually become the past. But all these ideas about time may lead physics to lose itself within psychological projection and self-delusion.

A prediction, using the opposites of alive/dead, would be that anything alive will move towards death, and all dead things will eventually become alive! This is quite obviously so if we think of the minerals (inorganic matter), which a body assimilates via plants to make them part of its expanding organization. It is also clear, that this organic body will later disintegrate to become 'life-less' atoms once again. This observation proves the strict separation between organic and inorganic matter as false. Organic and inorganic structures are one and the same thing, but appear as a different to the observer who cannot perceive the entire hierarchical cycle as the organization of a Oneness, which is the final form.

The duality alive/dead describes the Oneness of life as a continuum of fluctuating states. We live—we die—we live again! Once this is fully understood, questions like afterlife or past lives will be answered in the simple terms of duality fluctuation.

The duality of space (small/big), which creates the hierarchical range of any given form, can now be quantified by the principle of mutually attractive opposites. Free nucleus particles organize the atom, and those atoms sooner or later combine to form organic molecules, which form cells and organisms. Then the direction of movement reverses and the finalized structure becomes unstable and soon joins the substance of the Earth again, from which it all arose.

On a higher level, the inorganic structures also move towards spatial expansion, forming stars, galaxies and so on.

Will not, if nature adheres to her own principles and to a simple, self-perpetuating design, this 'inorganic' spherical organization on a macro-cosmic level behave in the same way as the microcosmic spheres—and move towards an organic form, from where it all disintegrates again just like all of observable nature does? Or should the opposite principle fail this once to work? Is the 'inorganic' expansion on the universal scale the purposeless point to life, love and poetry? Or wouldn't it be wiser to expect what we can observe to be indicative of a consistent larger purpose in nature?

If we can accept that the dualistic pair of organic/inorganic fluctuates according to the opposite principles, wouldn't it be sensible to expect organic life on a macro-cosmic level of the hierarchy?

To determine the purpose of polar reversal and the mechanics of the universe, we need to know but the precise polarity of its final form and the smallest building block.

The universal expansion is then determined by the final size, and the radius of the universe determines the speed of light as much as vice-versa. Consequently, the speed of the universal expansion today depends on the distance this motion still has to traverse before reducing the asymmetry of this universal cycle to O. It would follow that the speed of motion between dualities is proportional to the decaying polarity (or field) of the cycle.

On the atomic level we find the same principle at work: Because there is a proton and an electron, mutually attracted by being opposites, it should be possible to express the duration of this cycle in terms of the decaying electromagnetic field of the atom.

The principle of mutually attractive opposites is a wonderful tool in the hands of modern mathematics, since it allows all natural forms to be quantified as dualistic equations, where the motion between the poles defines their progress.

The four physical forces result from, and define the mechanism of this dualism expansion/contraction. Expansion includes all evolution of manifesting form and would be addressed as creation in conventional terms.

Physically, expansion includes the organization of form hierarchically, which is really all there is to expansion. Space is created by the hierarchical duality between small spheres and large spheres, and the hierarchy is created by the fluctuation between the smallest sphere of a form and its final size.

Evolution is to us the growing organization of form from stardust to the forms of today's universe. Our own life we see (from outside!) as a life-cycle, rather than as evolution. But the difference is purely relative, depending on the scale of the observer! The life-cycle of an organism appears, if observed from the level of micro-organisms, or even from the surface of a particle inside this organism, not like a life-cycle at all, but constitutes the evolution of thousands of generations of micro-observers.

Evolution and the life-cycle of a form are the same in principle, but appear different to an observer of any given scale, and different depending on the observer being inside or outside the observed object.

Creation eventually moves towards destruction/disintegration of form, and it carries the germ for this disintegration from the beginning. From proton-decay to the running downhill of all kinetic energy and the aging process of organisms, everything that evolves moves directly towards its own destruction. The destruction of the material manifestation of form is however not the undoing of form, but rather the means of its resurrection and the mechanism of its perpetuation. So can the continuity of form only be understood as based on a fluctuating duality, which is the exclusive cause for all cosmic movement.

However, just as every cause in a cyclical system moves towards its effect, every effect brings us eventually back to its cause. Causality is not a one-way street, but a symmetry! The physical forces do not only create the universe, but the form of the universe creates its own cause and the necessary forces as well, as everything creates its opposite in continuous fluctuations. Empirically, we can observe so little of the greater realities, which is why physics has so far only connected a few isolated pieces of the puzzle. If we want to perceive the Whole, we must not be distracted by detailed, tightly limited perspectives, but have to start with the first step that leads to knowing. We have to apply the laws we observe and make them part of our thinking, our method. When we plan to jump up in the air, a good idea is to bend our legs and lower ourselves first.

The principle of mutually attractive opposites sheds new light on a philosophical insight born of the same principle: The more we have come to understand and know, 'the more aware we become, that we know nothing...'

11. Symmetry fluctuations

'Every present state of a simple substance is naturally a consequence of its preceding state in such a way that its present is big with its future'
   -Leibniz -

The law of opposite truths could also be called the symmetry principle. It is the overwhelming principle in nature, mathematics and aesthetics.

Symmetry means in Greek, 'the same measure'—its etymology implying a repetition of measurable quantity. Symmetry is said to exist when a measurable quantity remains invariant under a transformation. The fluctuating symmetry of form is restored after every cyclical transformation, while the symmetrical parity disappears during the transformation. But here, the symmetry between design and final form is, as we have seen, not quantitative. Yet, the fluctuating symmetry of form is nevertheless the most fundamental symmetry that causes all other symmetries.

We have seen that it is possible to find previously unknown laws by looking for symmetrical relationships in nature. Einstein employed symmetry as a lamp to guide his way in the creation of new theories. In Special Relativity (which he originally called 'invariance theory,' he used the Lorentz transformations to maintain the invariance of Maxwell's field equations for observers in motion; in the General Theory of Relativity he did much the same thing for observers in strong gravitational fields. Wigner managed to organize all known particles in symmetry groups, classifying them according to their rest mass and their spin. Later Dirac derived the relativistic quantum equation of the electron, preserving the symmetries of both special relativity and quantum mechanics, and found that his equation mandated the existence of a positively charged electron, which led to the first intimation that there might be such a thing as antimatter.

The first gauge field theory beyond electromagnetism was then invented by Yang and Mills, and when Murray Gell-Mann took up the question of symmetry he soon developed the quark theory that sprang from it. For a while it was thought, that symmetry would explain all of nature's manifestations. Its intrinsic elegance and beauty was thought to be of divine perfection.

But there is this problem: by no means are all of nature's symmetries manifest. We live in a world where many of the observed symmetries seem broken! Young, working with Tsung Dao Lee, identified a discrete asymmetry in the weak force, called parity violation, and Glasgow spoke of the weak force and electromagnetism as linked by a 'broken symmetry!'

Research on spontaneous symmetry-breaking demonstrated that these events could create new kinds of force-carrying particles, some of them massive. It became clear, that symmetrical problems could have asymmetrical solutions, but still symmetry was seen as perfection and asymmetry as a broken perfection.

One particular asymmetry, showing that for every billion anti-quarks there was once a billion and one quarks, has been found to be significant: The few excess quarks destined to survive the general quark-antiquark annihilation in the early universe have formed all the atoms of matter in the universe!

Writing a fully unified theory will thus have to account for this shattering of perfect symmetry into the so-called broken symmetries of today!

Since we owe our very existence to imperfections of symmetry, it has to be asked if symmetry is really more perfect than 'broken' symmetry! If we envision a perfectly symmetrical universe, it will become quite obvious that this universe would be uninhabitable and absolutely sterile, since there can be no variance/evolution.

The solution to the problem of broken symmetries comes from the principle of mutually attractive opposites: If a system is symmetrical, it will fluctuate between its opposite poles, and while doing so—become asymmetrical for the duration of a half of its cycle. What is thought to be a defect or a broken symmetry is actually the polarity fluctuation that created the symmetry. Symmetry is never sterile or static, it moves constantly from one opposite to the other and back. The motion creating 'broken' symmetries is a manifestation of the evolving universe, of expansion, and the creation of form; it does not really break symmetry, but composes it with every new cycle.

Quarks can only exist, because 'up' quarks and 'down' quarks keep exchanging a gluon, tipping their balance from one asymmetry to another. The 'defect' of their symmetry is represented by the gluon, which is the vehicle of motion and the agent of continuity.

The unfilled outer energy levels of atoms are just such an 'imperfection,' but the bonding into molecules could not happen if there were a stable perfection of the atom!

This shows clearly how evolution, which requires molecular bonding, depends on the asymmetry created by the fluctuation of symmetry. With every symmetry-breaking event, evolution quantum-jumps towards the finalization of the universal form, and when the final form is complete, the symmetries will appear 'perfect' once again.

Symmetry + fluctuation = form + continuity

The existence of the universe can only be explained by the Oneness of form plus the broken symmetry of its polar fluctuation.

The human body works according to the same principle as far as its recurring form is concerned. But also its bilateral symmetry, as looking from front or back, is only near perfect!

The heart for example, just like the 'broken' symmetries of physics, initiates the movement of blood from left to right in a fluctuating symmetry. The nervous system is also a fluctuation of symmetry. The left part of the brain is the rational, logical aspect, while the right brain is intuitive and creative. Left could not exist without right, because there is no reason without intuition, and right could not be without left, since intuition without reason can never be fruitful. By processing information asymmetrically and passing it over to the opposite pole, our brain becomes capable of thought, and receptive to the surrounding dualistic reality. We can think only because the symmetrical parts of our brain are never in an exact balance, but constantly fluctuating between left and right. This is also the reason why learning is possible. Mental growth (= hierarchical organization of computed data) is to humans what expansion is to the universe...

The lungs are a duality that allows the moving of air, and there have to be two nostrils for that reason, where the left nostril has a different function from the right one. Inhalation through the right nostril warms up the body, while inhalation through the left nostril cools the body down, as is well known in the yoga-system.

The movers of fluid, the kidneys, the movers of sound, the ears, and the movers of light, the eyes, all obey the same principle. Everything we see is actually a fluctuation of two separate visual realities, observed from two different points of view. Hence, our very powers of observation are based on duality, and everything we see is therefore a picture made up of a duality fluctuation.

The various attempts at a unified Super-Symmetry Theory have sought to identify these symmetrical relationships by linking fermions and bosons—that is particles of half-integral spin, like electrons, protons and neutrinos, with those of integral spin, like photons and gluons.

If this can be attained, a fully realized super-symmetry theory would provide a unified account of all four forces and would shed light on the very early evolution of the universe as well.

The principle of fluctuating symmetries can fulfil these expectations, since it allows particles to be classified in terms of their function within the symmetrical fluctuation of the universal form! All particles participating in carrying the force of expansion will be the functional opposite of those particles that convey contraction. Photons are the conveyors of light = expansion, and gluons may convey the contraction on the universal scale. These particles of integral spin are fundamentally different in function from the particles of half-integral spin, like protons and electrons, which are building blocks of expansion without conveying it.

Gravitons convey gravitation in the evolving universe, and when the universe is fully expanded they will either change into gluons or be replaced by gluons, which carry the full gravitational potential of the universe down to the minimum level of expansion, which is the atomic nucleus.

Electromagnetism and gravity are the forces occupied with evolution/expansion, since they move towards finalization of the universal form, and the strong and weak forces collapse form by contraction and disintegration.

Each of the forces, and all of the participating particles, move towards their opposite and carry the germ of their opposite from the beginning. Therefore, particles exist in dualistic pairs like gravitons and gravitini, quarks and squarks, photons and photinos, and so forth. Gravitation already carries the germ of the strong force, to which it will eventually evolve, from the beginning of a cycle. And electromagnetism carries the germ of the weak force, which is its symmetrical function.

The main reason why this has not been recognized so far is that the forces seem to coexist at the same time.

Only if the mechanics of evolving form are considered, the functions of expansion and contraction can be understood as recurring fluctuations of generations of universes, where all the forces are present either as a growing potentials or as declining potentials. The fluctuation of such symmetries can be visualized as a wave function with constant minimum and maximum points. The polarity of fluctuating symmetries fits also what we define as a field, if not a magnetic field. But in a more common understanding it is simply the large cyclical movement of light, which is the vehicle of form, and which carries form not only to new projections, but throughout its life-cycles of hierarchical existence—without beginning and without ever getting lost or running down on fuel.

The so-called 'broken' symmetries are really the 'perpedo mobile' of perfect symmetry, and they alone allow symmetry to be continuous. After a transformation (full expansion of the universe), the symmetries are fully restored, but if observed during a transformation (still expanding universe), the symmetries seem 'broken' if they are not regarded in the context of evolving forces that will eventually reverse their identity.

12. Fluctuating symmetries and unification

Every physical change needs to break the symmetry between the energy before and the energy after the change, be it by exchanging a gluon, graviton, by emitting photons or generally by losing a token of energy which provides for the transmission. All change in nature happens by this 'breaking' of symmetries or in other words by the movement from one opposite of the polarity to the other, and back.

All known forces of nature in this universe can be expressed in terms of the one duality of expansion and contraction. Time and space are manifestations of this duality and have no separate existence apart from it. It should therefore be possible to express the four forces—gravity, strong nuclear force, electromagnetism and weak force—in terms of this polarity of expansion/contraction.

Let us suggest that gravity and the strong force are but two aspects of the One Contracting Force, and that their differences in strength and scale depend on the difference in geometry created by the expansion of the universe.

The expansion of the universe can be expressed by the differences in size between the universe as a whole and its smallest material building-block—the nucleon!

Gravity, which relates to mass, is proportional to a given aggregation of nuclei, which constitute practically all of the mass in matter. Gravity does hence act upon the nucleon.

On the other end of the universal expansion, we have the expanded size of the universe as it is today, giving the range of the present polarity created by expansion.

Now, in application of the principle of mutually attractive opposites, we can not only say that the nucleon has expanded itself to the size of the universe—but also that the contraction acts from the size of the expanded universe down to the size of the nucleon.

This means that the size of the expanded universe will determine the relative strength of the contraction, which is passed down to the minimum point of the polarity—to the nucleon!

Thus, the small is determined by the vast and vice versa, which describes a nature quite different from the linear evolution of cause/effect mechanics.

When the universal expansion evolves to the size of the universe, the resulting potential contraction, as measured on the level of the nucleon, is not negated by participation of the nucleon itself in the expansion, and will at any time be by just as much stronger than gravitation as the universe is larger than it was before it expanded from the size of a nucleon.

The force of contraction corresponding to the total size of the universe is localized at the opposite pole of the polarity created by expansion, which is the hierarchical level of the nucleon.

The strong force therefore ranges from the size of the nucleon to the even smaller level of the quark, but can, because of its polar direction, not act on the larger levels like gravity does.

Hence, it cannot surprise, that orthodox mechanics do not work on the quantum level or for the beginning of the universal expansion. Gravity depends on mass, given by the massive particles that shape space and evolve form. Gravity is a property of the massive particles, and the gravitational potential of a body is proportional to the amount of massive particles this body consists of. The strong force however is given by the potential contraction of the universe, which is the symmetrical result of its expansion, including its accumulated gravitational potential.

So rather than searching for the key of unification in the isolated geometry of the nuclear structure, it can be found in the symmetrical function of universal expansion/contraction!

The mechanics of form can now be quantified and proves accessible to mathematical verification:

The difference in strength between gravitation (relative strength = 1), and the strong force, (relative strength= 10^{41})

can be explained by the polarity of expansion/contraction, where each pole tends to act upon its opposite pole.

The range of gravitation is thus limited by the size of the universe, and the range of the strong force is limited by the size of the massive particles.

The nature of this polarity created by expansion explains why there cannot be a gradual, but instead a sudden demarcation between gravitation and the strong force, despite their coexistence on the quantum level.

The accuracy of these principles can quite easily be tested mathematically by relating the universal expansion (from the size of the nucleon to the size of the expanded universe of today) to the factor of relative strength between the strong force (10^{41}) —and gravity (1). If the size of the universe divided by the size of the proton gives us the same factor by which the strong force is stronger than gravity—this would be evidence for the proposed relationship between the forces:

A widely accepted age of the universe of 15 billion years can be assumed.

The radius of the universe is calculated as

1.3×10^{10} light-years.

The radius of nuclei $Tp = h/mp\ c \sim 10^{-13}$

1 Light-year equals 9.4×10^{12} Km

Radius of the universe / Radius of the nucleon equals

= 1.3×10^{10} light-years divided by 10^{-13} cm!

Radius of the universe / Radius of the nucleon =

$= 12.22 \times 10^{22} \times 10^{5}$ cm divided by 10^{-13} cm

$= 1.22 \times 10^{28} / 10^{-13}$

$= 1.22 \times 10^{41}$

We can now see that the ratio given by expansion proves indeed equal to the factor of relative strength between the strong force and gravitation! This shows quantitatively that the strong force is the origin and the result of gravitation, and that universal expansion alone explains the relative strength of the strong nuclear force!

The same correlation exists, when the age of the universe is divided by its age at the time, when particles were formed, which is approximately at 10^{-13} years of the early universal life.

$1.3 \times 10^{10} / 10^{-30} = 1.3 \times 10^{40}$ (where 10^{-30} is only approximate)

These simple ratios show the relationship between gravity and the strong force as being relative to the polarity of expansion/contraction of the universal form.

In a homogeneous, hierarchically organized nature, where each hierarchical level consists of smaller levels, and where the basic building blocks make up a whole—all forces are related and have the function of maintaining the duality of spatial and temporal expansion/ contraction, of which the hierarchy consists. Gravitation and the strong force are only separated by the factor of a single expansion of the fluctuating universal form, and so are the weak force and electromagnetism separated by a single contraction of the previous universe. This will become obvious, once the 'super-unified' theories take into account the Oneness of form and the duality of its mechanics.

13. The unsolved enigmas of the universe

Big Bang or Steady State?

We are now getting closer to understanding the universe in terms of form, but let us examine the existing theories dealing with the origin question in order to stay in touch with current cosmological speculation:

An expanding universe must clearly have once been very different from how it is at present. In the beginning, it is thought to have been very dense indeed, as dense as an atomic nucleus perhaps. Space was infinitely curved and all matter and energy was concentrated into a single primordial atom. This was the notion of George Gamow, who like Einstein had never lost his childhood curiosity and sense of wonder. His chief concern had to do with the formation of elements early in the history of the universe. He reasoned that the young universe might have been hot and dense enough for atomic nuclei to have been fused into various combinations, creating the elements as we know them.

This portrayal of a rapidly evolving plasma gave rise to the prediction of cosmic background radiation, a ubiquitous, simmering energy left over from the 'big bang.' At the time little attention was paid to Gamow's background radiation, but a decade later it showed up us a persistent hiss in several microwave receivers, and a Nobel Prize was won for this discovery. Today the assertion that we live in an expanding universe rests upon three fundamental lines of research. The first is the Hubble Law: The relation between the distances of galaxies and the redshift of their light have been found to be produced by the recession velocity of galaxies in an expanding universe.

The second piece of evidence is the cosmic background radiation which traces out the 'black body' curve that would characterize the spectrum of photons released by the big bang.

The third piece of data is chronological: The age of the universe, inferred from the expansion velocity, (some ten to twenty billion years), fits with the ages of the oldest known stars and with the temperature of the cosmic background radiation itself. The expansion of the universe had the tremendous impact of investing cosmology with a dimension of cosmic history. The structure of the universe, from that of atomic nuclei to the vast super-clusters of galaxies that stretch across hundreds of millions of light-years of space, could now be seen to have evolved from prior structures. What prior structures led to the event of the big bang became the big question for cosmologists who weren't afraid to think metaphysical thoughts. Others, adhering to the doctrine of causation, banished the issue of a first cause to exile in realms beyond science. As the astronomer Allan Sandage said: 'If there was a creation event, it had to have had a cause'. This was Aquina's whole question, one of the five ways he established the existence of God. If you can find the first effect, you have at least come close to the first cause, and if you find the first cause, that to him was God.

But can you go the other way, back outside the barrier and finally find the answer to the question of why there is something rather than nothing? No, you cannot, not within science....

So, to physics an incredible mystery remains: Why is there something instead of nothing? Despite such reservations, a few scientists tried to shed some light on how the universe might have originated. The Steady State Theory does not attribute the creation of all matter to one big explosion, but predicts that new galaxies are forming from atoms that are perpetually being created! Fred Hoyle, a highly original thinker and one of the brains behind the Steady State theory, came later on to the conviction that matter must have emerged from a state of high density and high pressure, as Gamow had always maintained. But on the other hand, there was much merit to the steady state, since we live in a universe of continuing activity instead of one that is uniform and inert. Instead of matter all the time becoming colder and more spread out, we often see it clustering together to produce the brilliant light of swirling galaxies and exploding stars. Why should this be so against expectations which appear soundly based in all other aspects of physical experience? Where is the drive for sustained activity coming from?

This important question is also avoided by the theory of 'Vacuum genesis.' To this theory, quantum vacuum is never really 'empty,' but instead roils with 'virtual' particles. Virtual particles are thought of as representing the possibility delineated by the Heisenberg indeterminacy principle, that a 'real' particle will arrive at a given time and place. Every 'real' particle is surrounded by a corona of virtual particles and antiparticles that bubble up out of the 'vacuum,' interact with one another, and then vanish, having lived on 'borrowed Heisenberg time.' A free proton, say, is not alone in its travels, but is surrounded by a corona of virtual protons, the existence of which influences its behaviour in ways that are not only observable, but are indeed fundamental to the interactions of the proton as we know it. It is the structure of the virtual particle clouds surrounding protons that make it possible for protons at the centre of stars to tunnel through one another's electrical fields often enough for nuclear fusion to be maintained. The quantum vacuum, then, is a seething ocean, out of which virtual particles constantly emerge, and into which they constantly subside. A vacuum so rich in potentialities cannot properly be called a void; it is really more like an ether.

The first physicist to think of vacuum genesis was Edward Tyron who drifted into a reverie when he was suddenly seized by the idea that the universe might be a vacuum fluctuation! Tyron's colleagues laughed and he put the idea out of his mind for years. Vacuum fluctuation, by introducing 'virtual particles,' is hinting at a creation caused by preexistent probability structures, which is the real virtue of the theory! On the other hand—it avoids the question of first causation, which is only extended to include the vacuum and its creative possibilities. But what causes a vacuum, or a virtual particle, to fluctuate and to trigger an ongoing creative process?

Spherical or hyperbolic, finite or infinite space?

Tyron realized that the overall energy content of the universe might well be zero. True, when one adds up the energy released by the big bang and by the starlight, plus the frozen energy that we call matter, that is bound up in the stars and planets, the total is an enormous positive sum. But there is also gravitation, which since it is purely attractive, belongs to the minus side of the ledger. Interestingly, the gravitational potential of the Earth, or any other object, turns out to be approximately equal to its total energy content as calculated

via $E=mc^2$. If this were true for the universe as a whole, then the universe would have no net positive energy and could have emerged from a vacuum without violating the law of conservation of energy. The question if the universe has zero energy, Tyron realized, depends on the rate at which cosmic expansion is slowing down. The rate of expansion is decreasing with time, supposedly due to the mutual gravitational attraction exerted by the galaxies upon one another. This at least is the mechanical cause, if only the known physical forces are considered. The rate of slowing therefore reveals the overall mass density of the universe, a quantity the cosmologists symbolize by the Greek letter omega.

If omega is equal or less than 1, the mass density is insufficient to stop expansion, and the universe will go on expanding, forever. Geometrically such a universe is described as 'open', meaning that the overall curvature of space is hyperbolic. If omega is more than 1, the expansion is destined eventually to stop, after which the universe presumably will collapse into another fireball. If omega is exactly 1, then expansion will continue forever, forever slowing but never quite coming to a halt.

Strangely, omega appears to be exactly equal to 1!

Cosmic space, so goes the conclusion, is therefore neither dramatically open nor dramatically closed, but is perfectly—or almost perfectly—flat. Of course, one could explain the flatness of the universe by identifying it as a prerequisite of human existence. The anthropic principle can explain the miracle of the flat universe, unless we imagine the creation of many universes, only a fraction of which chance to have the values requisite for life to appear in them. In so far as the creation of many universes cannot be tested, the anthropic principle may be a dead-end street. The English physicist Stephen Hawking, whose work is said to have contributed to the formulation of the anthropic principle, called it a 'counsel of despair.' The paradox of spherical or hyperbolic curvature then led Alan Guth to his hypothesis that the universe initially had expanded much faster than at the linear rate it evinces today. There had been an 'inflationary epoch,' he explained, during which the universe expanded exponentially. This meant that space was flatter and smoother by the time of the grand unified phase transition, and that far fewer mono-poles therefore were produced. So, if the vacuum was hung up in a symmetrical state during a phase of transition, after the 'breaking' of this symmetry, the universe would have undergone a brief period of very rapid expansion, after which it settled into the linear expansion rate that has characterized it ever since.

A Taoist simile may be drawn from water. Liquid water is more symmetrical than ice, and the change in water when it cools from a liquid to a solid state, marks a phase transition that breaks the symmetry. If liquid water is cooled very rapidly to below its freezing point, it will not congeal into ice at once, but instead linger in a liquid state for a while.

Similarly, in the inflationary universe account the cosmic vacuum remains empty even after falling below the temperature at which particle production ordinarily would take place. The latent energy is tied up in what is called a zero-value Higgs-field, which will inflate the dimensions of cosmic space, driving the expansion so that the empty universe balloons in perfect sphericity.

Inflation theory indicates that the universe is many billions of times greater in volume than had been estimated in the old big bang model. The observable universe, however, is thought to constitute but a fraction of the universe as a whole. Guth actually conjectured that creation need not necessarily be relegated solely to the past, but might happen again: If vacuum instability in our universe were to 'blister' in such a way as to form another universe, we would never know it. From our perspective, the only trace of the new creation event would be a pinpoint of infinite spatial curvature.

As it happens, there appear to be such places here and there, in the infinitely curved regions of space surrounding black holes! Conceivably, every time a great star goes supernova and its remnant collapses to form a black hole, it might give birth to a new universe, on the other side of space and time. Apart from the inflation theory, another idea, called 'quantum genesis' was put forward. Hawking explored the origin of the universe in terms of quantum probabilities and derived the quantum wave function of the universe as a whole. Noting that all world lines diverge from the singularity of genesis, he predicted the eventual collapse of the universe, and introduced the concept of imaginary time, which is the once and future time beyond expansion. Our time, says Hawking, is but the broken symmetry shadow of original time. When a hand calculator cries 'error' upon being asked the value of the square root of - 1, it is telling us, in its way, that it belongs to this universe and knows not how to inquire into the universe as it was prior to the moment of genesis.

Both of these theories can demonstrate deeper causes and more original early moves, but they don't solve the problem of the original first move and what prompted it. It seems, that just like the early expansion itself, the causes leading to these first steps are also leading to further causes and causes for those, according to the seconds we traverse in our approach of time 0. The paradox—hyperbolic or spherical—is still not solved by modern physics, nor is inflation theory, by acknowledging virtual particles or quantum probabilities, capable of answering the first move question.

The problem remains wide open, despite the various contradictory attempts of explanation in terms of either/or.

Oneness has evaded our either/or logic, and therefore the answers to the paradoxes of duality are still like echoes resounding from the realm where mind and cosmos meet.

Nothingness or infinity?

The possibility that the universe was generated from nothing, as soviet physicist Linde suggested, comes from the concept of the universe implying that nothing exists outside of it. This assumption is a direct consequence of the mechanistic dilemma that makes it impossible in principle to determine the first move by physical means. According to modern cosmology 'non-being' is described as follows:

'What is outside the universe is non-being,' or 'nothing can exist outside the universe.' This categorical negative is a typical example of either/or logic capitulating in the face of Oneness. The idea, that the universe must be infinite is a direct consequence of such an assumption.

It is thinkable, that the universe has also an infinite past, in which case an absolute first move will not exist. The thesis of infinity is of course not so much a solution of the problem, but enhances it. There is no scientific evidence to show that infinite time can always exclude the first move! The infinite thesis supposes that time is an infinite quantity, which also cannot be proven.

The paradox is, that assuming infinity, the problem of the first move is avoided, and supposing finiteness, the question of being from non-being cannot be answered by dualistic science.

Bounded or Unbounded?

The omega problem obviously has not answered the question, whether the universe is a limited one. If it stops expanding at some stage, so it is believed, it has to be limited. This is assuming that no other universes can exist. If it keeps expanding, it could be limitless in theory, but again only if no other universes exist that would form a boundary to a normally limitless expansion. The ideal of a limited universe seems to exclude the concept of a boundary.

While some mathematicians think they can prove the cosmos to be a limited one, others come to the exact opposite result. The emerging paradox appears to be unsolvable. Whether in ancient China or in ancient Greece, almost all the early models of the structure of the universe assumed it to be finite and bounded. This view has been subject to constant criticism. Finiteness, it is reasoned, means there is a boundary, and a boundary implies existence beyond. On goes the argument: Does a boundary have a beyond? If it does not, then this contradicts the notion of a boundary; if it does, then this contradicts the idea of the universe itself. For universe means everything and, so goes the gospel, there cannot be anything outside.

Aristoteles tried to solve this difficulty by saying that the inside is the physical space, while the outside is the world of Gods. Also Zhang Heng, a Chinese philosopher placed a non-physical existence beyond the boundary of a finite universe, thus resolving the contradiction.

Kant came to the conclusion that the universe can be neither finite nor infinite. Hence the finite-infinite question itself has no meaning and should not be discussed. However, Kant's unsolvable argument has implicitly used some unproven thesis. They are:

Finiteness must mean having a boundary.

Having a boundary must mean finiteness.

Infiniteness must mean having no boundary.

Having no boundary must mean infiniteness.

Kant thought these theses to be the most ordinary common sense that required no careful discussion. However, the above statements are not correct. In fact, having no boundary does not necessarily mean finiteness!

In the 5th century B.C., scholars thought if the Earth is finite, then surely people would fall off after reaching the boundary. In fact, the Earth has been shown to be finite but having no boundary. This is simply a property of spheres. The surface of a sphere is finite, but it has no boundary.

From the Earth being finite and boundless, to the universe being finite and boundless, all that is needed, is a slight generalization in geometry, namely a generalization from three to five dimensions.

If we suppose that the existence of matter is independent of position—and hence can endow space with a constant curvature—then, as long as this curvature has a positive value, however small, space can only be finite. Riemann's research has released us from Kant's impasse, and has shown that the finite-infinite question is not impossible.

According to the principle of mutually attractive opposites, it is actually quite impossible for infinity to exist without it moving towards its opposite and already carrying the germ of boundedness. As will be demonstrated in the next chapter, the universe can indeed be both finite and infinite at the same time.

The unsolved enigmas of cosmology are either/or problems, and their solutions do not come from a decision for either alternative. The riddle whether the universe is bounded or unbounded, limited or infinite, evolved from nothing or from something, is a reflexion of our inability to understand paradox as an intrinsic characteristic of Oneness and its dualistic mechanics. Whether the universe is bounded or unbounded is the wrong question to ask, as it disregards the opposite principle. The correct question is how the universe can be both bounded and unbounded. To our dualistic thought, this question is unusual and cannot be dealt with since it leads to the paradox of conflicting opposites. If however duality is understood as the mechanics of Oneness, the paradox disappears and points inevitably at this Oneness as the final answer to our questions.

In the Zen-tradition, paradox is used in the same way to arrive at the awareness of Oneness. By following the instruction of listening to the 'soundless sound,' the Zen student transcends ordinary learning and perceives reality as it is.

In physics we are using a slightly different method: Whether the universe is bounded, unlimited or infinite must be reduced to the single question: What form has the universe and towards which final form does it evolve?

To answer this, we will have to introduce the concept of form to our cosmological contemplations. The following chapter investigates form as the 'original singularity' from which it all sprang, and proposes a theory which solves the paradoxes of the early universe in a surprisingly simple way, without colliding with the established facts of empirical science.

14. Morphogenesis and the mechanics of form

The existence of the universe as a quantitative and energetic phenomenon can, as we have seen, be explained as a symmetrical polarity with a minimum and a maximum point of contraction and expansion, the various manifestations of which are but aspects of each other. This is how far as observation, relativity of size, and logic based on linear cause and effect can carry us.

Unexplained by dualism alone is however the existence of form of and within the universe! There is a very, very obvious fact of reality that can easily be overlooked in physics, as it seems to belong in biology: It has to be quite clear that the universe consists not only of quarks, atoms, stars, galaxies, and clusters—but also of life-forms like animals and human beings, including all their products! Computers, space-rockets, plastic chips and electronic music are all part of nature in this universe, and contribute much of the forms existent in the universe, which all on its own has developed every-thing we can think of. It would be hard to try and explain all the phenomena of life, including human behaviour, in terms of mechanistic views, in exclusively physical terms, or by randomly chosen probabilities! Even if physical or chemical factors that determine a pattern of differentiation can be identified, the problem still remains of how these factors are themselves patterned in the first place, to achieve just this same result. The critical point is—life-forms are as much a hierarchical level of universal structure as are spiral galaxies! Much more so—if galaxies, like atoms, serve to form the tissue of just such life-forms that reach their complete form just beyond the super-cluster systems...

Mechanistic theory states that all phenomena of morphogenesis are capable in principle of being explained in terms of the known laws of physics. This is the basis of modern day materialism, which denies 'a priori' the existence of any non-material causal agency, as well as the almost complete ignorance in humans—of actual reality. The physical world is considered causally closed, and conscious experience is seen as material states of the brain. This is how we are—either this or that!

According to a modified philosophy of materialism, the universe is composed of matter and energy, which are either eternal or of unknown origin, organized into an enormous variety of 'inorganic' and organic forms which all arose by chance, governed by laws which cannot themselves be explained. All human creativity, like also evolutionary creativity, must ultimately be ascribed to chance. Human beings adopt their beliefs (including the belief in materialism) and carry out their actions as a result of chance events and physical necessities within their brains. Human life has no purpose beyond the satisfaction of biological and social needs, nor has the evolution of life, nor the universe as a whole any purpose or direction. This assumption of materialism, that only matter is real, is still upheld by corporate scientists, who look for a justification to continue thinking within the established framework of thought provided by existing physics and chemistry. To attribute every-thing to chance is of course essentially non-scientific, and it denies the possibility of an obviously purposeful nature as much as that of a human failure to understand this purpose. Since material particles have come to be regarded as forms of energy, there can be no justification to uphold any materialistic philosophy, nor a mechanistic world view, as the first cause is always purely energetic and the original design never explainable by the physical forces. To imagine a complexity to exist without being designed is quite irrational and has no place in science.

In order to deal with Oneness-problems like the origin of form, or the first move, physics as a 'pure' science cannot on its own give a solution in conclusive or comprehensive terms, but needs to reunify with all other branches of human thought.

Only Oneness can recognize Oneness—that too is obvious!

At this point we must examine the various separated schools of thought, like biology, psychology and philosophy, and allow for a unification process to take place that considers the existence of life within physics, the influence of mental states on the microcosm, and generally the motives and purposes of interactions between energy and matter.

Since the mind of the observer plays a decisive role at the quantum level, it invariably influences every aspect of reality! The interactionist theory postulates that mental phenomena need not necessarily depend on physical laws, but rather follow laws of their own. The psychoanalytical schools see many aspects of behaviour and subjective experiences as depending on the subconscious or unconscious mind. In order to account for the facts of waking experience and of dreams, the unconscious mind has to be endowed with properties totally unlike those of any known mechanical or physical systems. C.G.Jung provides this thought on the collective unconscious: 'In addition to our immediate consciousness, which is of a thoroughly personal nature and which we believe to be the only empirical psyche, there exists a second psychic system of a collective, universal, and impersonal nature which is identical in all individuals. This collective unconscious does not develop individually, but is inherited. It consists of preexistent forms, the archetypes, which can only become conscious secondarily and which give a definite form to certain psychic contents!' Jung tried to explain the collective unconscious physically by suggesting that archetypal forms were 'present' in germ plasm. Within the scientific world, it was however never accepted, that archetypal forms could be inherited chemically in the structure of DNA.

Parapsychology has for a long time been considered an area in which superstition, fraud and credulity are rife. The scientific research of paranormal phenomena has found many cases that could be explained by normal causes, but numerous experiments designed to test for extra-sensory perception and psycho-kinesis have yielded positive results with odds against chance coincidence of thousands, millions or even billions to one. From a mechanistic point of view, these phenomena ought not to occur, or they are believed to depend on laws of physics 'as yet unknown.' The interactionist theory can only make slightly more sense of it by supposing the phenomena depend on 'non-physical causal factors' or 'connecting principles.'

These thoughts and theories all flirt with the truth, but lack the conclusive simplicity that makes it all comprehensible.

Several theories are based on formulations of quantum theory involving 'hidden variables' or 'branching universes,' and postulate that mental states play a role in determining the outcomes of probabilistic processes of physical change. Vitalism claimed that living organisms imply an 'additional' causal factor beside physical laws, and Driesch argued that the fact of regulation in biology made any machine-like system inconceivable. Driesch believed, that a non-physical causal factor acted on the physical system but was not itself a part of it. He called this factor entelechy. He postulated that entelechy organized and controlled physio-chemical processes during morphogenesis. The genes were responsible for providing the material means for morphogenesis—the chemical substances to be ordered—but the ordering itself was brought about by 'entelechy.' Driesch described entelechy as an 'intensive manifoldness,' a 'non-spatial causal factor' which nevertheless acted into space. He emphasized that it was a natural (as opposed to a metaphysical or mystical) factor, which acted on physio-chemical process. It was not a form of energy, and its action did not contradict the second law of thermo-dynamics or the law of conservation of energy. He suggested, that entelechy acted by affecting the detailed timing of micro-physical processes by 'suspending' them and releasing them from suspension whenever required for its purposes.

One has to compare these theories about living forms with cosmology and physics to notice how much the descriptions overlap!

According to Heisenberg's uncertainty principle, positions and timings of microphysical events could be predicted only in terms of probabilities. By 1928, the physicist Sir Arthur Eddington was able to speculate, that the mind influences the body by affecting the configuration of quantum events within the brain through a causal influence on the probability of their occurrence. Unless it belies its name, probability can be modified in ways which ordinary physical entities would not admit of. In physics, matter is energy, and organized by mind (the 'observer') –which is why cosmology is able to ask where the universe came from. Physics must now ask the same questions we ask in biology when we seek what design or cause beyond matter may determine an organism. Why? Because physics cannot just abstain where it comes to describing the microcosmic reality inside a mouse—or the quantum-probabilities of thought-processes! Specialization must never mean leaving vital areas of the human experience to other 'specialists,' by excluding them entirely from one's own perspective. The physics on the atomic level inside a living mouse surely cannot be less fascinating than the physics of a piece of uranium, or the inside of a meteorite! We may feel just a little silly once we notice how much the atomic worlds inside the mouse are determined by the complete form to which they assemble—determined by its will, its feelings, its behaviour—and not very much by our non-hierarchical laws of physics!

Physics needs to take a good look at the endocrine galaxies of dopamine, serotonin, adrenaline, thyroxin, and all those other chemical compounds for what are in our human reality simply—feelings! To a tiny observer—they are galaxies! Of matter! Galaxies of matter that are to a higher level of the hierarchy feelings of joy, alertness, fear or anger! This may be confusing to the engrained specialist—but there cannot be any fruitful science in any field, without this understanding that specialization must constantly alternate with unification, and that all realities overlap. Only from this unifying perspective can we see that form in physics, including the universal form, follows the precisely same rules as do the living forms we know on our planetary level. Physics and biology do not describe different subjects at all. Physics simply looks from the inside, while biology looks from the outside at a complete form!

The question of what form the universe takes when observed from outside, urges us to discover when and how it originated. 'Entelechy,' or 'non-spatial causal factors' lead us straight into mythology, if not vagueness. They basically assert that physics does not apply where the spiritual begins, which is an illusion based on division and specialization. Everything physical can have a soul, and every spirit may well wish to incarnate. But for a physical universe to begin, its eventual physical form needs to be 'known' from the start. Why introduce a 'chreode'—if we have seed that knows the form of a tree; if we have quarks that know the design of the universal form; if we have a mama-dog that explains the puppy-universe?

15. Morphogenetic fields and archetypal germs

While quantitative factors in physics, like mass, momentum, energy, temperature, pressure, electric charge etc., can be measured and expressed mathematically, forms can only be represented visually. They are simply themselves and are recognized directly, as long as the observer is outside the complete form.

Form is not a vector or scale or quantity, nor does it seem to be conserved. For example, if a tree gets burnt to ashes, its form simply disappears. While scientific activity is concerned mainly with the empirical testing of mathematical models dealing with quantities, form could never be explained in terms of numbers and the problem of where form comes from is still as little investigated as ever.

However, it can be shown, that form is not a function of matter at all, and does not depend on the presence of what we commonly call matter. If we close our eyes and visualize an apple, the form of an apple appears exactly as if the physical apple were present. Also in dream states forms are present quite independently of physical matter. This proves that form is not produced by matter, but has an existence that includes both the material world and the non-material world. If form is not caused by the physical forces or by matter, is it then a preexistent singularity, and unrelated to the cause and effect relations of this physical universe?

The question of how the universe came into existence is a morphological problem, and therefore has to be addressed in terms of morphological concepts. The idea of 'formative causation,' borrowed from biology, could lead to a singularity of archetypal form capable of explaining the physical forms of the universal structure and the form of the universe itself. It is quite helpful to visualize Sheldrake's morphogenetic fields, in order to appreciate 'hierarchy' and the mechanics of form, which he seems to approximate.

According to Rupert Sheldrake, a morphogenetic field can be thought of as a structure surrounding or embedding the morphogenetic germ, and containing the virtual final form; this field then orders events within its range of influence in such a way that the virtual form is actualized. Morphogenetic fields differ radically from electromagnetic fields in that the latter depend on the actual state of the system—on the distribution and movement of charged particles—whereas morphogenetic fields correspond to the potential state of a developing system and are already present before the system takes up its final form! This exact perspective needs to be applied to cosmogony! After the final form is actualized, the continued association between the morphogenetic field and the system whose form corresponds to it, will tend to stabilize the latter. Aggregative morphogenesis occurs progressively in inorganic systems as the temperature is reduced: As a plasma cools, subatomic particles aggregate into atoms; at lower temperatures atoms aggregate into molecules; then molecules condense into liquids and finally liquids crystallize. In the plasma state, the naked atomic nucleic can be regarded as the morphogenetic germs of atoms; they are associated with the atomic morphogenetic fields, which contain the virtual orbits of electrons. In one sense, these orbitals do not exist, but in another sense they have a reality which is revealed in the cooling plasma as they are actualized by the capture of electrons. In atoms with many electrons, each orbital can contain only two electrons, then the orbitals with the next lowest energies, and so on, until the complete atomic form has been actualized around the morphogenetic germ of the nucleus. Atoms are in turn the morphogenetic germs of molecules and so forth. If it seems rather artificial to think of chemical reactions as morphogenetic processes, it should be remembered, that much of the effect of catalysts, both organic and inorganic depend on their morphology! For example, enzymes provide surfaces, grooves, notches or basins into which the reacting molecules fit with a specifity which is often compared to that of a lock and key. The morphogenetic germ is provided by this pattern itself. It is well known, that the addition of 'seeds' or 'nuclei' of the appropriate type of crystal greatly accelerates the crystallization of super-cooled liquids or supersaturated solutions. The action of the morphogenetic field of a morphic unit on the morphgenetic fields of its parts, which are morphic units at lower levels, can be thought of in terms of the influence of this higher-level probability structure on lower-level probability structures. Consequently, during morphogenesis, the higher-level field modifies the probability of probabilistic events in the lower-level morphic units under its influence. Thus, the morphogenetic fields of molecules restrict the possible number of atomic configurations which would be expected on the basis of calculations which start from the probability structures of free atoms. And this is what is found in fact: in the case of protein folding, for example, the rapidity of the process indicates that the system does not 'explore' the countless configurations in which the atoms could conceivably be arranged.

Morphogenetic fields of atoms should not be considered to have a privileged position in the order of nature; they are simply the fields of morphic units at one particular level of complexity. In living organisms, as in the chemical realm, the morphogenetic fields are hierarchically organized: those of organelles—for example the cell nucleus, the mitochondria and chloroplasts—act by ordering physio-chemical processes within them; these fields are subject to the higher-level fields of cells; the fields of cells to those of tissues; those of tissues to those of organs; and of organs to the morphogenetic field of the organism as a whole.

This theory of Rupert Sheldrake seems, since we have seen the inorganic and the organic worlds to be essentially one and all phenomena intrinsically connected, quite capable to explain form in and of this universe, and can even be applied to answer the question of how it all began. If morphogenetic fields are hierarchically organized, that would mean that all forms we encounter in the universe, have been ordered by the higher-level forms from beyond the known universe!

If we can accept that something like morphogenetic fields is responsible for the forms we know, it would be common sense to reduce the convolution of it all by simply knowing that form generally is passed down from higher hierarchical levels, and that the forms inside this universe are determined by the influence of a 'morphogenetic field' from a higher hierarchical reality—which is quite simply the universal form!

In the light of this realization, the moment of the 'big bang' can be seen as that stage in the continuity of universal form, where the universe was a morphogenetic germ, starting to evolve towards its final form by creating the forms inside itself that have been ordered by the higher-level 'morphogenetic field', which was the previous universe.

Atoms assemble to form molecules, organelles, cells, tissues, organs, living organisms, planets, star systems, galaxies, clusters of stars, universes....

This processes which we have come to see as evolution, do not move in one direction only! The organization of the universe from small to large defines a polarity, and as such must also move towards its opposite. This means that the reproduction of form onto progressively larger levels, starting from the morphogenetic germ of the quark, is not all there is; the reproduction of the large forms, which acts from the largest scale down onto the morphogenetic germ, is equally a part of the entire creative process. This contraction part of form is how the 'chreode', the 'field', passes itself down the hierarchy.

The morphogenetic germ evolves towards its final form, as ordered by the' field' of this final form, and the final form itself contracts towards the morphogenetic germ by the very process of ordering it.

The idea of the morphogenetic field and the morphogenetic germ nicely illustrates the polar principle and the mechanics of form as we have discussed it, since it recognizes the basic duality of morphogenesis, where the small is determined by the large and the large is determined by the small. If we see the universe as the morphogenetic field, which orders the atomic nucleus to evolve towards the final form of the next universe, the universal form becomes a self-regenerating system of minimum and maximum manifestation. But what does this really achieve in terms of an explanation?

When we consider the form of our universe, the morphogenetic field seems an unnecessary complication of a far simpler reality: The form of this universe is but a new generation of a previous universe, which provides all the necessary ingredients for a new cycle of evolution towards the final form to occur. But let us be simple here:

It would not be 'wrong' to see the tree as the morphogenetic field which orders the seed to evolve that then grows towards becoming a new tree—but the morphogenetic 'field' cannot be quantified, tested or used to predict the evolutionary behaviour of form. All that is needed is a tree, not any 'field' of that tree, for its seed to have direction, expansion, and detail of design! Living forms do however all have electrical fields, even magnetic fields, whether they are plants, animals, or humans—and if a field is what we seek, the aura surrounding living things may well serve to convey their morphological reality. But the 'field' is still completely ordered by, and emanating from the form itself.

Evolution is on a larger temporal and spatial scale the same thing as the life-cycle of the forms we already know, and the morphogenesis of evolving species is part of the universal cycle. On the universal scale, there is likely no need for morphogenetic fields, since form itself provides the maximum point of expansion which orders the minimum point of expansion to evolve towards its final form.

The dualistic mechanics of form explain morphogenesis on the universal scale quite without the introduction of fields, as a continuity of self-perpetuating form! This sheds an entirely new light on the known principles of evolution, and the idea that atoms follow the patterns given by higher-level forms convinces far more than Darwin's random selection, competition and survival of the fittest. The existence of form within this universe and of this universe need not be explained by formative causation, since this theory is not concerned with the universal form or with cosmogony, and because a field is not needed for form to reproduce. It is limited to a narrow spatial and temporal scale, and can therefore not recognize evolution in terms of the hierarchical mechanics of form. The idea of a morphogenetic germ must be replaced by the form of the universe as it is carried over into this universe, from the previous one, that is the blueprint. This implies, that the atomic nucleus, or rather the quark, carries with it the design for the final form of the universe, just like the seed carries with it the design for the mature tree. If this is so, the final form of the universe can be known from the characteristics of its parts, and it must certainly be every-thing contained by any of its parts.

The universal form must be as simple as its simplest part, and it must be at least as complex as the human mind and as sophisticated as a living organism, for its form to order those characteristics.

16. The organismic universe

The question of what the form is that the universe grows towards provokes the decision of whether to expect it to be an inorganic whole or an organismic one. The universe has in modern times always been considered as inorganic and dead—an explosion. Mainly a self-reflection of the materialistic modern mind, this view seems confirmed by our observations of heavenly bodies like the stars and galaxies that obviously fit our non-hierarchical definitions of 'inorganic' or 'dead.'

It is however time that we asked questions like whether organic and inorganic molecules can really be discerned at all, and whether they fit separate definitions altogether. It would be tempting to just follow the vitalists' concept and look for a 'vital spirit' that inhabits living organisms and enables them to perform activities that cannot be carried on outside the living organism—but it is also a flight into mysticism!

On the hierarchical scale, it is quite a task to identify activities of life, or even to visualize the form of a complete universe. For the moment, it may suffice to borrow the mechanistic view that sees the living body essentially as a machine; the arms and legs move like levels, the heart like a pump, the lungs like bellows, and the stomach like a mortar and pestle. The question is, whether the universe as a whole, could be such a 'machine' that qualitatively would have to be addressed as an organism, a biological machine.

This will depend on whether or not the chemistry of living organisms is governed by the same principles as the chemistry performed in a laboratory. The 'reductionists' believed, that complex operations of living systems could be reduced to simpler and more readily understandable ones, and they achieved a partial victory, when the German chemist Friedrich Wohler converted an inorganic substance (ammonium cyanate) into a familiar organic substance (urea). Today it is generally believed that living systems 'obey the rules' of physics and chemistry. As depreciative as this may be in the qualitative context of life, it still shows the acceptance of a basic sameness between organic and 'inorganic' building blocks. Factually a living system is made up mainly of water (50-95%).

Small ions such as K+, Na+ and Ca2+ account for no more than one percent. Only the rest is composed of what we call organic molecules. Organic molecules are molecules containing carbon. It now can be asked if the galaxies, clusters and super-clusters that make up the macro cosmic universe, can indeed be 'molecules' of an organic system.

It would of course be insufficient to say, that since there can be no water flowing around in space and since we cannot prove a cluster of stars to function as a carbon molecule in a living system, there cannot be such a thing. We must remember the incredible vastness of space and our relative position as an observer. A water molecule for example would be so large relative to us, that it cannot resemble what we call water in the least. It would not even look gaseous from nearby, but simply like round heavenly bodies separated by vast, empty space.

Similarly, the biologically important elements, carbon, hydrogen, nitrogen, oxygen, phosphorus and sulphur would be so large in scale, that we may find it hard to identify them by their known characteristics. Structures seem quite different if projected on such large scales, and what we call a physical state, for example the liquid state, loses all meaning if observed from our scale.

Relativity of hierarchical scale needs to be applied to understand this—if an observer stands on the surface of a proton within an atom of a water molecule, his analysis of water would not identify it as being liquid, but instead he would be surrounded by empty space and see electrons as the sun and the stars of his sky, and he would see his universe as fiery rather than liquid.

A good indication of whether the universe as a whole is an organic system or a lifeless machine can be obtained by the availability of the necessary elements of life, even on our scale of molecular form. If for example carbon exists only in isolated pockets, this would make it unlikely for any large-scale carbon to be readily available throughout the universe. If however the universe contains the molecules of life on the small scale, evenly distributed throughout the universe, it can be said to have at least the blue-print and the availability, which makes a repetition on higher levels probable due to hierarchical repetition of form.

As a matter of fact, we do find the biologically important elements throughout space and not just on this planet. Carbon, the most important one, is generated in stars, and supernova explosions scatter carbon throughout space.

The universe is a factory of biologically important elements, which means, that it fulfills the chemical requirements of being 'organic.'

The omnipresence of hydrogen, which is the main element to fuel the stars, seems like the small-scale equivalent of the high percentage of water contained in organic cells. At first, it may appear that lifeless atoms have little to do with biology. A closer look however reveals that the activities we associate with being alive depend on combinations and exchanges between atoms, and that the force that binds the electron to the atomic nucleus stores the energy that powers living systems.

A remarkable discovery concerning the existence of life throughout space has been made by several scientists who could show, that meteorites contain particles which appear to be fossilized organic materials! It has been confirmed, that bacteria are remarkably similar in size to interstellar grains and that these particles in space have an abnormally low refractive index, just as bacteria have when they are thoroughly dried.

A study of the particle sizes obtained from more recent comets was published in 1981 by a group of Japanese astronomers, where particles were typical of bacteria, and in the same year, American astronomers showed that cometary particles emit exactly the kind of radiation that would be expected from organic material. Some micro-organisms like the bacterium Micrococcus radiophilus withstand the massive doses of radiation in space and survive its low temperatures and pressure. These abilities would be completely wasted on Earth and there would be no reason whatsoever for them to develop. For cosmic life however, these are essential requirements.

Fred Hoyle in 'The intelligent universe' demonstrates how viruses that come from space can actually combine with human genes, so that parents infected by the virus will produce young with added genes, because the new genes added by the virus are copied together with the previous genes whenever there is a cell division during the growth of the offspring. A process therefore does exist, whereby the genetic structure of a species is continually modified, not by adaptive mutations, but by genes from outside the Earth!

If new genetic material is reaching the Earth all the time, it can be said that much of the DNA of every planet and animal will consist of alien, or universal, space-traveling genes.

This means not only that the universe is indeed filled with the principle of life; it also shows that this life is in a constant communion and inter-connectedness with our life on Earth and of course—that the universal form influences the evolutionary processes of humankind via genetic 'messaging.' If the genetic pool of humankind is constantly influenced by genes from space, we can only deduce a fundamental interconnection between the human evolution and the purpose of the universe as a whole! This same connectedness exists also right here on Earth, where the chemical substances extracted from plants have an intimate relation to chemical processes within humans. Morphine, for example, interacts strongly and meaningfully within the human nervous system. Quinine interacts both with the human system and with the protozoon that causes malaria. Penicillin, originally extracted from a fungus, has an enormously beneficial effect in treating a whole spectrum of human diseases.

The juice of the king-coconut is even interchangeable with human blood plasma. Close correspondences like these are inexplicable in terms of conventional biology in which the genes of such widely separated species are required to have evolved quite independently from each other.

The similarities are explained, however, by the same cosmic genes being present in both plants and humans! Fred Hoyle did not see life in our galaxy as a collection of isolated pockets, but as a coherent Whole developed out of a single aggregate of cosmic genes—and he was, as we will find out, quite correct.

The nature of any system can at least structurally be understood by observing the patterns of its composite parts. So can also our entire universe be recognized by the hierarchical patterns it consists of. Indeed, it can only ever be comprehended in terms of these patterns, the structures of which are determined by the entire system. It is blatantly certain that we live in a comprehensible universe, and that the means, objects and horizons of our studies are representative of the wider reality, the All of it. If we can recognize the universe by that which we can actually observe, there can be no doubt that life is part of the equation. The very fact of our existence, and that of plants and animals, proves that parts of this universe are organismic—a fact easily overlooked by specialized physics. These living parts of the whole are structural participants in the entire system—part and parcel of what the universe is in essence. This is so easily missed because we see ourselves as the neutral, separate observers of a universe that is out there. But in actual reality we are totally connected within this larger living system, and its living manifestations are all around us and inside us, despite the far away stars, of which our size tells us, that they are dead and unrelated to us...

What appears to be dead from our perspective is really just as alive as any single part of any organism is alive. Each atom in our own bodies had its origin in that enormous beginning fifteen billion years ago, which is the birthday of this universe. We accept, that we are made of flesh and blood, but, here goes the paradox—we are also stardust! The same paradox has to apply for the universe as a whole.

It is for this reason that ancient astrology saw the stars as related and connected to the fate of humans and why many people still believe this to be true, despite the failure of astrology to provide convincing material evidence.

17.The Cosmic Egg

Considering the firmly established model of a mechanistic universe of dead matter from twentieth century science, it seems a daring quantum jump to proclaim this universe to be a living organism and its functional parts to be connected, purposeful, and relating to the existence of life.

But this is the strength of the Cosmic Egg theory—cosmological observations can be tested against known biological facts like growth-rates, reproduction-cycles or metabolic changes! We will therefore propose a theory which in our mechanistic times walks the borderline between physics and philosophy, but which fits precisely with the observable physical and biological facts, and which can explain the so-called paradoxes of cosmogony in a simple, consistent, and conclusive way.

The form of the universe, let us propose, behaves like every other form in our experience. It has a minimum from where it grows toward a maximum, and this minimum 'knows' on the quark-level how to unfold the hierarchy—and reach its maximum!

A close look at what expansion means in biological systems reveals how the universe really evolves!

The principal key to the secrets of the universe has always been the phenomenon of light, and with it the expansion at the speed of light.

This key lost its shine with the comparison of expansion with an explosion. Naturally, the great heat in the beginning, and the speed of expansion would, in a mechanistic model of the universe, and for an observer limited by his size, provoke the comparison with what we know as an explosion. The problem however is, that speed and temperature are on a cosmic scale not at all what they seem to be on our scale, and the speed of expansion allows perfectly for a comparison with a developing, growing organism on a cosmic scale! The concept of an expanding universe is very new to modern cosmology and therefore the implications of expansion, and of its speed relative to observers on various hierarchical levels, have not been discussed in a biological or even a hierarchical context.

Western cultural history does not contain any inkling of universal expansion. Even Einstein regretted that because he could not shake off the influence of tradition, he had narrowly missed the opportunity of discovering the concept of universal expansion himself.

The New Zealand Maori however describe the creation event as the separation between Rangi, the Father of heaven, and Papatuanuku, the Earth-mother after Conception; after the state of Oneness. An ancient chant translated by the Rev. Richard Taylor in Te Ika a Maui starts with the first period of Creation, the genesis of thought:

From the conception the increase,

from the increase the thought,

from the thought the remembrance,

from the remembrance, the consciousness

from the consciousness, the desire.

The universal expansion is here a consequence of conception and it leads to thought on a universal scale. Although the pre-creation period kore, which is defined as an all-pervading Nothing, very similar to the Tao of the Chinese and the emptiness of the Zen-Masters, there are still hints of earlier generations of Gods before Rangi and Papa... Constantly reappearing periods of blackness, nothingness, or death suggest a cycle of birth and rebirth of Gods. Descendant Gods like Tane, or Maui seem to represent mankind and remind us of Gods like Prometheus or Christ. Basically, we have generations of Father/Mother/Child, which serve to explain all of Creation from Nothing—kore. In ancient China as well, there was no lack of intuitive comprehension about the expanding universe and the meaning of it.

For example, in San Wu Li Qi (the three-five calendar),

Xu Zhen wrote about Creation and expansion:

Heaven and Earth are all mixed up like an egg, and Pan Gu is born therein. After eighteen thousand years, Heaven and Earth separate. The clear Yang becomes Heaven and the murky Yin becomes Earth, and Pan Gu is in the middle, undergoing nine changes every day. The spirit is in Heaven, the sage is on Earth. Every day Heaven rises by one zhang, and Earth sinks by one zhang. Thus, for eighteen thousand years, Heaven becomes exceedingly high, Earth exceedingly deep and Pan Gu, exceedingly tall. Hence, Heaven is ninety thousand li from Earth.

This vivid theory of universal expansion is not only qualitative; it is also quantitative. Let us check the numbers. If on each day Heaven rises by one zhang, then the distance between Heaven and Earth increases by two zhang each day, and each year it increases by 2 x 365 = 730 zhang. According to the ancient Chinese system 1 li = 300 bu = 150 zhang.

Hence the yearly increase in the Heaven—Earth separation is 730:150 = 5 li. Hence, if 18000 years have elapsed since the 'separation of Heaven and Earth,' the present distance between them should be:18 000 x 5 = 90 000 li. This is precisely the figure given by Xu Zhen, who must have given the matter some careful consideration.

We can use exactly the same method to calculate the age of the cosmos given by the modern theory of universal expansion: Galaxies at a distance of 10 million light-years from us have an outward velocity of 150 Km/s. We might rephrase this as Heaven rises by 150 Km every second!

Since 1 light-year = 9.4×10^{12} Km

1 year = 3.16×10^7 s,

150: $(9{,}4 \times 10^{12}) \times 3{,}16 \times 10^7 = 5 \times 10^{-4}$ light-years/year

i.e. Heaven rises by 5×10^{-4} light-years every year.

Thus, the time taken to reach a distance of 10 million light-years is:

$$T = (1 \times 10^7) / (5 \times 10^4) = 2.0 \times 10^{-10} \text{ years.}$$

This is the counterpart to Xu Zhen's eighteen thousand years. Certainly, it can be asked, if T is the time required to achieve 10 million light-years, would not the time be longer for a greater distance? It is however agreed for the law of universal expansion, that the speed of expansion is proportional to the distance. For example, objects twenty million light-years away will be expanding at 300 km/s and so the time taken to reach 20 million light-years is again T. In short, objects today at various distances would have been piled together about

2.0×10^{10} years ago. We derive the following conclusion: All objects observed today have a finite age, which is no greater than 20 billion years (1 billion = 1 thousand million).

This beautiful example of ancient intuitive science has been handed down and put into a modern cosmological context by the Chinese scientists Fang Li Zhi and Li Shu Xian, whose thoughts are barely known today.

Is it not surprising, how Xu Zhen arrived at these quantitative results thousands of years ago? More surprising however is the fact that modern science, even where it appreciates the quantitative precision of these statements, nevertheless chooses to ignore the qualitative part! Xu Zhen clearly describes the universe as an egg, containing an embryo! Since this vision doesn't fit with western traditional beliefs, it is simply ignored as a primitive or superstitious explanation. It is however very unlikely, that Xu Zhen should have been able to calculate the growth of the universe so accurately—and on the other hand is dealing in fairy-tales and primitive metaphors! It would be far wiser not to preclude the possibility that his description of the universe as a connected Whole describes the truth as accurately as do the figures! Xu was, after all, a few thousand years ahead of western explanations and he was not kidding at all when he described the universe as an egg, and Pan Gu as born therein!

In the context of living nature all around us, it makes a lot more sense to recognize the expanding universe as a living thing rather than as a big explosion. Everything makes suddenly sense that was until now a mystery, a paradox, or a black hole of speculation!

How could a dead universe evolve and contain such intricacies as plants and animals; or know intelligent life like human beings or trigger-fish? Of course, the mere fact that such a dead universe cannot satisfy our desire to find some purpose of life on a higher plane must not be a reason to assume it to be a living universe. But if we aspire at all to extract overall knowledge from those parts of the universe we can actually see and understand—we have to consider the reality of living forms as significant, even fundamental, to the universal form! Assumptions, like there being nothing outside the universe, are contradictory to any observation we can make within our immediate reality where there is always something outside of every-thing. Throughout time our perspective of the universe has been expanding. Each time we discovered a new planet or particle, humankind followed a tendency to hold on to narrow descriptions of a small universe. When it was first suggested that the Earth was not the centre of the cosmos, with the sun rotating around it, there was fierce rejection of any such heresy. This human tendency has never really changed in principle and today, with the discovery and description of galaxies, clusters and super-clusters of stars, it is still just as difficult for us to make any-thing of those vast numbers. Even to cosmologists the increased range of the universe means hardly any-thing in a qualitative way. Quantitative science has given us figures of sizes and distances, all having to do with billions or trillions of entities, but to our qualitative awareness, the universe has not become the slightest bit more comprehensible. We can still only imagine this planet Earth to contain life and a multiplicity of form, and we see form in our range of observation as coincidence rather than as typical for the manifestation of reality on all levels of existence. The images we have seen of a barren moon and mars, and the scientific speculations about the improbability of life on places unlike Earth, have also helped to drive us into the assumption that we live in a basically dead and random universe, and that the universe is nothing but an explosion of energy and matter, unrelated to life and unrelated to humans.

In ancient history, we still thought of the Earth as the centre of every-thing and humankind the as crown of creation. With the discovery of the wider universe this idea was given up as a delusion, supposedly based on self-important views, and in our modern day it is considered primitive or naive to try and give humankind any role of importance in a mechanistic universe.

Today, all we see are mathematical figures on quantitative phenomena which most people don't bother with—and any reference to the human condition is banned from the realm of pure physics. Since all things tend to develop towards their opposite, it seems that our view of the universe has done just that—where in the past our perception of the universe was quantitatively quite erroneous, it qualitatively still was seen as the human environment, as including humans and relating to them. Now, we have moved towards quantitative accuracy, however meaningless, and at the same time towards a qualitative nihilism. Humankind has completely lost its place in a universe as described by modern science. It may seem like an ego-less enough attitude to think of ourselves as unimportant in the context of spatial vastness—but really, this vastness emphasizes only the very special position of the human form! Our trust in quantitative science has no more to do with modesty than the ancient respect of humankind for itself had to do with primitive self-importance! As a matter of fact, the ancients may well have been right after all in considering the human form as the most central and fundamental principle of all! It may have been intuition rather than self-importance to disregard the quantitative aspect and to go by the obvious. Even if we live in a vaster universe than any-one can imagine—why should the human principle lose any of its qualitative importance just because of its diminutive manifestation on this scale? But the impossibility to visualize astronomical scales—differences given by the hierarchy—has a major impact on our psychological ability to perceive the universal form! The universe is still imagined as 'all there can be,' and the speed of its expansion, as observed from our hierarchical level, makes it difficult to even contemplate the idea that the universe might have a form at all. And, of course, the emptiness of space as perceived from within the universal form promotes this illusion that the universe is synonymous with mystery and infinity. Yet, the physical universe is just as limited in space as are the super-clusters and any other physical form, and its size should not distract us from its physical and morphological reality! The actual form of the universe simply cannot be compared with the form of a star or a galaxy or any microcosmic building block. It is rather a complete unit—which was the reason for the assumption it had to be all there is. In a sense, this is correct, because the universe is not one of many universes, like a star is one of many stars that make up a galaxy. The universe seems to be all there is if observed from inside, and no visual aid will ever detect any-thing outside of it. This phenomenon is however not a mystery, nor is it unique, if we consider the known hierarchical levels within our range of vision! Certainly, if we stand on the surface of a planet, we will be able to see the stars and other planets. This is however different for an observer within one of the hierarchical spheres. On the cell-level of the hierarchy a micro-observer inside the cell would perceive his universe as growing, bounded and as all there can be, since the cell-membrane forms an impenetrable boundary that hides every-thing that is outside. This observer might also have a vague notion of infinity, of 'parallel' universes, and of larger, seemingly meta-physical realities. But physically, the content of his cell-universe is all he may ever conceive of by empirical means. The molecules of his cell will appear like galaxies of stars, gradually drifting apart, while the cell grows—and he will ask himself the same questions we ask ourselves about the origin and the finality of our universe.

It is highly unlikely, even morphologically impossible, that the system of universal organization produces atomic systems, star systems, galaxies and so forth in a hierarchical repetition of the same spherical form—while living forms should be unique and unrepeated throughout the entire system! The mechanics of form don't allow for a sudden appearance of form on a single level of the spatial hierarchy, but recognize form as a hierarchical continuity between a minimum and a maximum. Therefore, the organic levels have to be repeated also—on other levels of the hierarchical system!

The Cosmic Egg theory consequently suggests the known structures of the perceived universe to be atoms and molecules of a macro-cosmic level of organismic reality that takes the form of a cell. It thus reconciles the innate intuition of ancient and more sensitive humankind with the quantitative facts of cosmology. It admits that the universe is from a mechanistic point of view very much as cosmology describes it, but recognizes it as a universe that fundamentally relates to the human form, and returns to humankind its ancient place at the centre of all things. Any morphological 'fields' become unnecessary to explain a universe that like any other living form is created by the reproductive means of genetics!

This explanation reconciles every religion, from the sun-cult and Christianity to the veneration of the Earth Mother, with modern science, as it cleanly solves all the unsolved paradoxes of cosmogony simply by focusing on the mechanics of life rather than on the darkness of matter.

It is not overly surprising that modern theories have not come up with the idea that the universe might be a living body, as there are seemingly obvious reasons for this to be quite impossible and far-fetched. We will look therefore at these reasons of 'impossibility' before contemplating the grounds for the correctness of this theory.

The seven strongest arguments against the universe being organismic are:

1. The emptiness of space
2. The speed of expansion
3. The heat of the stars
4. Exploding stars
5. The closed universal system
6. The lack of essential elements
7. No molecular bonding

Empty space:

The emptiness of space seems to contradict any notion we have about organic tissue, and therefore the idea to compare between the two does not occur. Even the fact that space is found to be not all that empty after all, but rather just less densely filled with matter, does not make it look any less lonely and frightening. However, a study of relativity shows that there is no difference at all if we compare it with a cell or a molecule. If an observer on the surface of a proton within a human cell looks out at his surroundings, he is faced with exactly the same emptiness of space. The distance from one proton to another, or from a proton to an electron, is just as vast, and the space in between just as empty as the macro-space we are looking at through our telescopes, and yet—the observer is inside a cell, looking at its cellular structures! The difference between the observed structures is therefore simply relative to the size of the observer and to his position within the hierarchy. An observer looking from within a proton would again have a totally different version of the universe. This difference is not one of scale, but one of position or dimension. Relativity and quantum physics cannot explain the nature of the universe as such, but can only give feedback in terms of our projections and of the particular position the observer occupies. Data about the laws of nature are therefore meaningful only relative to a particular observer's position, and become distorted or inaccessible if applied without hierarchical consideration to the design of the organized structure. The emptiness of space does hence strongly confirm our analogy with the inner empty spaces of organic tissue.

The speed of expansion

The reason why human observers consider the expansion of the universe to be fast enough to compare it with an explosion is twofold. Firstly, the speed of light is as fast as any explosion we know, and secondly the high initial temperatures of the early universe also remind us of an explosion. Since organic tissue is not in a state of explosion, it does not seem to fit the analogue. But let us consider some hierarchical Relativity: The speed of light may always be the same, no matter how fast an observer moves, as Einstein confirmed. But it is not the same to the experience of an observer on a different level of the spatial hierarchy! The speed of light does not change, as long as we measure in kilometers per second of your scale, but whether this seems to be fast or slow, depends on the size of the observer. Since humans cannot go and change their size, this problem seemed never of any practical relevance. However, the mechanics of form as explained in this theory make the question of Hierarchical Relativity very relevant indeed. To the human observer the speed of light, which is the speed by which the form of this universe grows, is the top limit of possible speed, which makes the fifteen billion years of universal expansion at the speed of light seem like a long, long time. But how does it appear to an observer larger than the universe? To the time-experience of this super-large observer the total expansion of the universe may be but the time he needs to take one step across the diameter of the universe! Given the slower growth rate of an organic substance as compared to the movement of the observer, he will actually have to wait for a while if he wants to watch the universe grow from beginning to full expansion! To this observer then, the speed of light would be nothing like it is to us. It would rather compare with the rate of organic growth on his own time scale. On the other hand, the growth-rate of a human ovum, if observed by an observer of comparably minute size, would similarly move with fantastic speed!

The universe is 10^{26} times larger than a human observer $(10^{28} / 10^2)$—so in order to find the comparable size of the tiny observer within the ovum (10^{-3} cm) the same ratio will give the size of 10^{-29} cm for the tiny observer. This is smaller than any-thing we have yet been able to discern.

The observer of size 10^{-29} cm lives in a time much faster than our own, and the cell seems billions of his years old. The growth-rate of this cell will seem incredible to this observer. If the cell grows by 10^{-4} cm a day of our time, this will be 10^{25} times the size of the tiny observer.

In other words, while the cell grows a little in our view, it expands to the relative size of a universe, if experienced by the small scale observer.

But, will some say, the growth of a cell is not constant as is the expansion of the universe, and it is eventually going to stop expanding. According to the inflationary universe theory there was however at least that one brief period in the early universe, when the expansion unfolded a lot faster than it did later. This gives us the first indication that the universe does not expand in a constant way! The reason, why human observers experience the universe as expanding at a constant rate today is the limited time frame that we can actually observe. Even looking backwards in time by observing very far away star-clusters can only give us information on an average expansion rate, but does it allow for a detection of sudden 'quantum jumps' in expansion, or for a few slight accelerations and decelerations as it is typical for the growth of a cell? If it were possible to test the speed of expansion for long periods throughout the life of the universe, it would have to be described as almost constant, just like that of a growing cell. An important piece of evidence for this phenomenon is the deceleration of the universal expansion! It is generally accepted, that the universe will indeed expand to a predetermined size, where it will stop growing. To our view, this is due to deceleration caused by the gravitational potential which will eventually suffice to keep all matter in the universe from expanding any further. But no matter how it can be explained in mechanistic terms—the fact remains that the universe will eventually stop growing, to take on a definite, bounded size. This final size is not predetermined by 'vacuum fluctuation' or by any forces as physics knows them. It is simply the size to which the universe will grow to achieve its final form. It may be possible to find rather precise analogues when comparing the growth of an ovum in its early stages to the universal expansion. But of course, there is no reason to assume that the great universal cell will grow at a precisely proportional rate to the cells on our scale. It suffices to show, that there is no fundamental difference that could prevent a comparison. If we explain the expansion and the deceleration of the universe with the physical forces, we can do the very same thing regarding the growth of a cell, which also employs the forces of nature. Fact is, that both the cell growth and the universal expansion are not quite, but almost constant, and that they are limited to a predetermined final size, when growth/expansion will stop. The observed difference in speed is a result of the relative position of the human observer in the hierarchy of space/time and not an absolute reality. Therefore, the expanding universe can very well be a growing cell as far as speed and the predetermined range of expansion are concerned.

The heat of the stars:

Another apparent problem in identifying the universe with an organic system consists in the great heat of the stars. It can be calculated that the temperatures at the core of the sun are about fifteen million degrees, which would destroy all organic tissue on our scale of the hierarchy. As pointed out earlier, time, space and temperature are not absolutes, but aspects of each other when seen in the context of their hierarchical position. If the temperature on the cellular level is 37^0 Celsius

for humans, that does not mean that on a 10^{26} times larger scale this same absolute temperature will be found in organismic structures. Temperature is very relative in this sense. Our temperature requirements for life to exist mean nothing when translated into a cosmic hierarchical reality. The large distances between the stars actually distribute the overall temperature in the cosmos to a quite comfortable level, if seen from a universal perspective. The same is the case within the human body, where the individual atomic particles don't measure 37^0 of temperature! What the universe and the cell obviously have in common is far more compelling: Both produce heat and maintain equal warmth throughout the system! A cell has, no matter how large the scale, a need for equal distribution and a constant maintenance of warmth. If the universe does not fulfil this requirement, it cannot be a cell. We have learned that the stars are not like a bomb, although nuclear fusion is the same mechanism that functions in a thermonuclear weapon. When a chain reaction occurs in one tiny area in the centre of a star, it does not normally touch off other reactions in the surrounding gas; instead, the additional heat expands the gas slightly, lowering its density and so decreasing the probability of further proton-collisions for the moment. Owing to this self-regulating process, as averaged out for countless interactions, the entire star equilibrates, expanding to damp the rate of thermonuclear process when they can attain a runaway rate, then contracting and heating to increase the rate when the centre begins to cool. This mechanism endows the Earth and the whole universe with constant warmth and life. Throughout space we can detect another piece of evidence regarding a maintained temperature level—the cosmic background radiation! To our understanding a temperature of only three degrees Kelvin does not seem much, but on a cosmic scale, things look different. We can't know exactly how background radiation temperature and the dispersed heat of the stars translate into the temperature requirements of the cosmic cell, but the fact, that such temperatures are maintained throughout the entire cosmos is quite remarkable, no matter how we rationalize and explain the phenomenon functionally. If we find a physical cause to explain such 'coincidences,' then so will we find the physical cause for maintained warmth in organic bodies. Moreover, we detect not only a background radiation supplying the cosmos with an equal distribution of warmth, but the stars, too, are distributed equally—so that the temperature in no part of the cosmic system can drop below what might be regarded as the required level of cosmic warmth. To explain this fact with strict causation, like equal expansion in all directions, cannot deny its functional significance, since the warmth of a cell could be explained in exactly the same way. A cell produces heat by the means of chemical reactions—and so does the universe. Both distribute warmth throughout the system and maintain the required equilibrium. The comparison of absolute temperatures has to be seen in the context of spatial hierarchy and cannot be directly applied. From an anthropic point of view, it would be nonsensical to doubt the benefits of the stars' heat—since it is obviously the heat of the sun which makes organic life as we know it possible. The secret is in the right distance, which is the key as to why the heat of the stars on a cosmic level cannot be considered hostile to life.

Exploding Stars:

It is difficult to imagine how supernovae can fit into the context of organismic cosmic life. A supernova can occur if a star of about ten times the mass of our sun becomes unstable enough to explode. On our compressed scale, where each hour equals a billion years, all these spectacular stars die within the first few minutes. Conceivably, their explosions may shock any remaining gas in the cluster into collapsing to form new stars, but any giant stars produced in this fashion will also consume themselves quickly. These supernovae could well play a role in the chemical processes of the cosmic metabolism, or they may simply be a self-regulating mechanism preventing instabilities within the cosmic molecular make-up. Supernovae are actually indispensable to life on our scale as far as nucleo-synthesis is concerned. To fuse iron nuclei, the heat of normal stars does not suffice. The production of iron requires intense energy, and the nuclei of still heavier elements like Technetium and Californium consume energy rather than releasing it. Therefore, stars could not do the job and still shine. Supernovae are factories of these heavy elements, of which iron is essential to organic life. They have the function of manufacturing this essential element without which life could not exist. However, for the generation of materials on a cosmic scale, supernovae may not have great significance. The iron and other elements they produce belong to our planetary scale of molecular structures and cannot directly account for the supply of a universal cell. Supernovae, as dramatic as they may seem on our scale, mean no more than a flicker of radiation within an atom of a molecule in the cosmic cell. To imagine an exploding star to be incompatible with organic tissue on a cosmic scale is therefore quite unwarranted.

The Universe—a closed system?

A cell is not a self-sufficient system. One of the criteria by which we identify living matter, ranging from prokaryotes to the most complex multi-cellular eukaryotes, is that it exchanges substances with the 'non-living' world. This occurs at the level of the individual cell and is accomplished by the cell- membrane. Control of these exchanges is essential to protect each cell's integrity, and to maintain those very narrow conditions of pH and ionic concentrations at which its metabolic activities can take place. In addition to the cell membrane, which controls the passage of materials between the cell and its environment, internal membranes, such as those surrounding mitochondria, chloroplasts, and the nucleus, control the passage among intracellular compartments. Of the many kinds of molecules surrounding and contained within the cell, by far the most common is water. Furthermore, the many other molecules and ions important in the life of the cell are carried in an aqueous solution. Therefore, our consideration of transport across cell membranes will focus on how water moves. In both the animate and 'inanimate' worlds water molecules move from one place to another because of differences in potential energy, usually referred to as the water potential. Water moves from a region where the water potential is greater to a region where it is lower, regardless of the reason for the water potential. An example is water running downhill in response to gravity. Pressure is another source of water potential, and it can exceed the water potential produced by gravity. In solutions, water potential is affected by the concentration of dissolved particles. In the absence of other factors (such as pressure), the water potential of a solution is directly related, to the concentration of water molecules. A particular instance of diffusion—that of water across a membrane that separates solutions of different concentration—is known as osmosis. Diffusion is a familiar phenomenon. If one sprinkles a few drops of perfume in one corner of a room, the scent will eventually permeate the entire room, even if the air is still. Substances that are moving from a region of higher concentration of their own molecules to a region of lower concentration are said to be moving down a gradient. A cell oxidizes fuel-molecules for energy. As a result, there is a higher concentration of carbon dioxide inside the cell than out. Thus, a gradient is maintained between the inside of the cell and the outside, and carbon dioxide diffuses out of the cell down this gradient. Conversely, oxygen is used up by the cell in the course of its activities, so oxygen present in air or water or blood tends to move into the cells by diffusion, again down a gradient. Similarly, within a cell, molecules or ions are often produced at one place and used at another. Thus, a concentration gradient is established between the two regions, and the substance diffuses down the gradient from the site of production to the site of use. The question is whether the universe as a whole can, as assumed by cosmologists, really be a closed system, or whether it gives any hints of letting objects in and out! From our position, it is not yet possible to observe the cell-membrane, or the outer rim of the universe. So, the only way to detect any movement of substances that may leave or enter the system is to look out for any deviations from the general direction of the movement given by expansion. Regarding transport of materials within the system, it has to be asked if a process similar to diffusion can be detected.

Materials produced by stars and supernovae seem to be distributed throughout the universe exactly by such means of pressurized diffusion! The intense pressure created by stellar explosions creates enough diffusive potential to transport materials to other places in the universe. Additionally, the materials will have a tendency to move down the gradient from the high concentration in the star to the low concentration every-where else. The kinetic potential created by the pressure from explosions is sufficient to overcome even the gravity of the star and send materials in every direction. Where-ever these materials are needed, they are recollected by the means of gravity. That this is not a random phenomenon is emphasized by the fact that every part of the universe is supplied and that the materials are indeed traveling from where they are produced to where they are needed, down a gradient. The stellar material is, as pointed out earlier, possibly not sufficient in scale to supply the cosmic cell with the energy it needs, but in this case, there is no reason why, according to hierarchical repetition, the same system should not be in effect on a super-galactic level as well. The known facts suggest that the transport of materials through the system is driven by 'diffusion' both in the cell and in the universe.

The more central question however is, whether this universe admits new materials from the outside and whether any-thing ever disappears from the universal system. According to the inflationary model of the universe, the first particles suddenly appeared from a vacuum, from 'nowhere,' since space did not exist. This thesis is an attempt to explain the paradox of existence from non-existence. It is in this respect highly unscientific, since it uses a metaphysical dogma to hide an obvious dilemma. What the idea of vacuum genesis really suggests, is to ignore where the 'virtual' particles come from, in order to avoid the admission of an open universe, which would threaten the core of mechanistic faith. The idea of a vacuum-fluctuation is a very desperate attempt to explain every-thing in terms of matter and it closes the door to our perception of the universe as an open system, connected to parallel and prior systems. The purist determination to avoid metaphysics at all cost, and the religious faith in a mechanistic framework, have led us to a head-deep plunge into a premature metaphysical 'first move' that becomes more mysterious the more it is mechanized. Rather than explaining the sudden appearance of 'virtual particles' with the religious term of 'nowhere,' we could for once stick with actual logic and conclude that the 'somewhere' is outside the known universe! If the universe is perceived as an open system, the paradox disappears, and the virtual particles are explained in terms of interactions between the inside and the outside of the universe. Owing to quantum indeterminacy virtual particles still do materialize out of space all the time. We don't know how exactly they accomplish doing this, but the conclusion is there: Rather than endowing the vacuum with divine qualities of creation, we have to face the fact, that these virtual particles appear from outside the system of the universe! Virtual particles that suddenly enter this universe don't come from non-existence, but from not perceived existence! The cause for this sudden and unobservable appearance is the cell membrane and the gradient of potential energy given by the demarcation of density between the universe itself and the outside. If the universe is recognized as not only growing, but also as open and sustained from the outside—all false mysticism disappears from cosmogony. Metaphysical thought should never compete with science or replace it where we face the unknown; it should instead accompany science wherever we appreciate reality.

Once the fact is established that materials do enter the universe from the outside, we can easily accept the possibility of larger materials, as needed by the cosmic cell, entering the system via similar pathways. It is conceivable that all materials enter the universe as 'virtual particles,' but it cannot be excluded that even entire galaxies enter the universe via quantum jump from the outside.

There is also evidence for materials disappearing from the cosmic system! Even large objects, like stars, can, when they come too close to a 'black hole,' simply disappear! They get sucked into the black hole and vanish! Mechanistic theory would provide for this disappearance by reducing it to a shrinking caused by gravitational pressure. But the mass of a star caught in a black hole is believed to be conserved, just like that of the black hole itself. A more functional explanation would be, that a black hole evolves to become a tunnel out of this universe, in some cases out of a specific region of this universe, and that materials caught by the black hole get sucked right out of this universe. I am suggesting that black holes, because of their high concentration of matter, create a process of diffusion out of the universe, down this gradient, while 'remembering' the mass debt, created by the assumption that this universe is all there is!

Another model for the case of active transport could compare a black hole with the sodium potassium pump, a transport protein that reacts like a revolving door. And yet another possibility consists in the comparison with endocytosis or exocytosis, in which substances are transported in vacuoles or vesicles composed of portions of the cell membrane. Taking into account the highly concentrated mass within a black hole, the possibility of active transport seems rather remote. It shall therefore be suggested that substances leave the universe via black holes, by the means of a cosmic 'diffusion' down a gradient to the lesser concentration of mass outside. These exchanges of materials keep suggesting that the universe is a living system that maintains its organization and structure just like any living cell. This should not surprise the naturalist who knows from experience that a closed system cannot exist any-where in nature. The Earth is an open system also, as it receives an energy input of 13×10^{23} calories per year from the sun. A theory that sees the universe as closed would make it a universe that cannot be understood by its observing and observed parts, which are all open systems, and it would make all scientific effort futile in principle.

To comprehend the universe as open, on the other hand, avoids the contradictions with all of observable reality within this universe.

A lack of essential elements:

Of the ninety-two naturally occurring elements, only six make up some 99 percent of all living tissue. These elements are carbon, hydrogen, nitrogen, oxygen, phosphorus and sulphur. All of these elements need to gain electrons to complete their outer energy level, and thus they form covalent bonds. Because these atoms are small, the shared electrons in the bonds are held closely to the nuclei, producing very stable molecules. Moreover, with the exception of hydrogen, atoms of these elements can all form bonds with two or more atoms, making possible the formation of the large and complex molecules essential for the structures and functions of living systems.

On the cosmic scale, the essential biological elements can be formed by entire galaxies, and they probably form covalent bonds through the mutual attraction we call gravity! This needs to be tested by comparing, for example, the mass of individual galaxies and relating it to the atomic weight of those elements. Covalent bonds in which electrons are shared unequally are known as polar covalent bonds, and the molecules containing these bonds are said to be polar molecules. Such molecules often contain oxygen atoms, to which electrons are strongly attracted. The polar properties of many oxygen-containing molecules have very important consequences for living things. For example, many of the special properties of water (H_2O), upon which life depends, derive largely from its polar nature. Since water on a cosmic scale appears to us as having far lower temperatures than on the planetary scale, it will take on the appearance of being frozen! Therefore, and because of the size of its molecules, water on a cosmic scale must seem to us like any other molecular structure. The bonding situation is different in another familiar substance, carbon dioxide (CO_2). When two double bonds are made by a single carbon atom, as in carbon dioxide, the three bonded atoms lie in a straight line. The symmetry of the carbon dioxide molecule has an important consequence: The double bonds, like all covalent bonds between non-identical atoms, are polar. However, because the molecule is perfectly symmetrical, the electrons are pulled in opposite directions by the two oxygen atoms, canceling out the unequal distribution of charge. As a result, the carbon dioxide molecule is non-polar. This can give cosmology a clue for how to differentiate between different groups of galaxies in terms of their polarity! Another clue is the number of spiral rings around a galaxy and their mass. Assuming that galactic groups make up structures proportional to our molecular structures, it may be possible to determine the exact nature of the cluster we inhabit in terms of molecular identity. Possibly, the spiral rings of a galaxy are the equivalent to the orbits of electrons and may reveal similar purposes. All we know for certain is the fact that the most important elements for living systems, carbon and hydrogen, are readily available throughout the universe. It seems reasonable to assume, that the grouping of stars does not follow haphazard and purposeless patterns, but that it is, as with atoms and molecules, organized in a functional and purposeful way. Nature is simply consistent, and the cosmic structures have to have a chemistry-like function, if Creation is to be understood as having as much purpose on the macro-cosmic scale as it clearly has on the smaller scales.

No molecular bonding?

In an organic universe, all the stars should be found to organize themselves much like atoms and molecules of our scale, and there should be interactions similar to the chemical reactions in a living cell on the known scale. This requires, assuming the same laws of molecular bonding apply on a cosmic scale, that galaxies form structures like atoms, capable to interact with other atoms by the means of ionic bonds or covalent bonds, or a technique similar to those. Firstly, it has to be quite clear that stars on their own are not comparable to atoms in their function or relative size. Assuming the same proportions between an atom in a cell as we know it, and an 'atom' of the cosmic cell, it would have to be the galaxies that function as atoms in the universal cell, which remains so far speculative.

Except—a cell is about 10^5 times bigger than its composite atoms—and the universe is also 10^5 times bigger than a galaxy!

If we look at the spiral arms of the Milky Way system, a strong resemblance to the orbitals of electrons becomes apparent! At a given energy level, an electron moves around the nucleus at almost the speed of light. The electron is so small, and moves so rapidly, that it is considered theoretically impossible to determine, at any given moment, both its precise location and the exact amount of energy it possesses. As a result of this difficulty, the current model of atomic structure describes the pattern of the electron's motion, rather than its position at any given moment. The volume of space in which the electron will be found ninety percent of the time is defined as its orbital. Similarly, the Milky Way, as any other spiral galaxy, has a core around which rotate what we call its spiral arms.

The spiral arms of the Milky Way seem to fit the definition of orbitals, which are the volume of space in which the electron is found 90 percent of the time. They also allow for a linear understanding of how electrons move from one level to a higher one without needing to resort to quantum jumps from one level to another, 'without traversing the space in between!' The Milky Way appears to have four such orbitals and could form a Potassium (K), or Calcium (Ca), or Iron (Fe) atom on a cosmic level. If it could be confirmed that the core of the Milky Way consists of nineteen or twenty composite parts, which are the atomic numbers of potassium and calcium, this thesis could be verified.

A difficult question to answer is how galaxies exchange 'electrons' in ionic bonds or covalent bonds, in order to form molecules. No-one has ever observed such a galactic quantum jump and possibly it cannot be readily observed from our position. How could one, in the case of ionic bonds, detect the Milky Way to become electrically charged, for instance? Many observations on this scale simply cannot yet be made. However, we know the phenomenon of 'eclipsing binaries', which are double stars, so close together in the sky that they look like simple stars even through the most powerful telescopes. They happen to be oriented in space in such a way that they periodically eclipse each other. The resulting variations in the total brightness of the system bear a superficial resemblance to genuine variable stars, which change their brightness owing to internal pulsations. Similar phenomena could occur on the galactic level, and it would be even less noticeable. Nevertheless, such periodical eclipses can, on a galactic level, constitute a sharing of electrons as needed for molecular bonding! On the other hand, it could be even less accessible quantities like the so-called 'shadow matter' or the 'dark energies', that play a role in molecular bonding. It is to be hoped, that empirical research will provide us with data that can enable us to elaborate on this particular subject—once the relevant questions are asked. Another possibility is that gravity itself serves as a mediator of molecular bonding. Obviously, galaxies do group together to form clusters—just like atoms form molecules. This formation to clusters is ascribed to the gravitational force, but it should not yet be excluded, that on the galactic scale gravity may function as an agent of interaction to bond galaxies together like atoms are bound into molecules. It is after all gravity which attracts the materials of which the spiral arms of the Milky Way are made from space. This exchange is mutual, since a galaxy can, like also a single star, send materials into space, that will eventually be recollected by another nearby galaxy. But gravity can only account for the attraction of the spiral arms around a galaxy, to the core, not for the molecular bonding itself. The better question is, whether something like electromagnetism can be detected to act between the core of a galaxy and its spiral arms.

The greater the amount of energy possessed by materials in the spiral arms of a galaxy, the further they will be from the core. Exactly the same principle applies for electrons and for planets. But while planets can move to an energy state in between orbits when energy is added to them, electrons can't. For an electron to move from one energy level to a higher one, it must absorb a discrete amount of energy, equal to the difference between two particular energy levels. This discrete amount of energy, called quantum, seems to be needed in the galactic system as well, in order to lift materials into an outer arm of the spiral. Otherwise there could be no clear demarcation of such arms which define the precise orbitals materials have to occupy when rotating around the galactic core. It should be asked whether electrons might move on spiraling orbitals as well, just like the spiral arms of a galaxy! A quantum seems to be the amount of energy needed to propel substances through a spiral fast enough to appear on an outer arm of the spiral. Hence, the electron appears to 'jump' from one orbit to a higher one, when really it moves along a spiral pathway. If we introduce a spiral model of the atom, the galaxy becomes comprehensible as a big atom where the spiral arms are the orbitals of electrons rotating around a nucleus, which is the core of the galaxy. The strange idea of an 'instantaneous' quantum jump, without traversing the space between the orbitals soon clears up when the orbitals are seen as spirals: An object moving along a spiral actually reaches an outer orbit without traversing the space between the spiral rings, and it also needs a discrete amount of energy to reach an outer ring. The whole phenomenon of instantaneous quantum jumps is well explained by the spiral model of the atom without a need for miraculous disappearing acts and sudden rematerializations of electrons. The electrons simply move gradually along their spiral orbitals, and when they appear on an outer ring they seem to suddenly have jumped from the inner ring to the outer one. With galaxies, this same process can be studied at a far slower pace. Their orbitals or spiral arms can actually be visualized by photography, whereas the behaviour of electrons is extremely elusive. If we consider the persistent grouping of galaxies, not only to clusters, but to so-called local groups, we cannot reasonably avoid drawing the conclusion that galaxies form structures similar to the molecules of our scale. Gravitation alone, much less any other physical force, cannot explain this phenomenon despite its omnipresence in the universe. The molecular bonding of galaxies does not seem to differ much from that on our scale. The spiral arms of galaxies appear to have a similar function as the 'orbitals' of electrons, and the galaxies are factually grouped together in a way that could not be explained in any purposeful way but by the process of molecular bonding and the exchange of substances between the galaxies of a local group or a cluster. For these reasons, we will hypothesize the universe to be organismic, and cellular. What still remains, is the question of what form exactly the universe takes, or else to what organism the cosmic cell belongs.

18.Consciousness and the quantum projection of form

The most incomprehensible thing in the universe is that the universe is comprehensible! (Einstein)

Apart from the biological principles we have explored to explain the universe in terms of its parts, there is still one phenomenon about the observed universe which is to be considered paramount—the observer!

In the anthropic view, physical laws are gradually built up in the course of man's study of cosmic phenomena. Therefore, physical laws must possess the property of being comprehensible to man. It is indeed unimaginable, that a dead universe of random evolution could ever be understood by humans! The very existence of the human being supports the idea that humans can only exist in a living universe that is intimately related to man! The basic idea of the anthropic Principle is this: the reason why the universe is as it is, is because if it is not so, then there will be no humankind and nobody to become conscious of the universe. In brief, things present are so because man exists at present. This logic is very different from a disconnected mechanistic view which holds that the existence of the universe and the existence of human beings in the universe are unrelated. Even if the mechanistic view still enjoys a resigned popularity today, it must be quickly discarded for the most obvious of reasons. How can a universe which has produced human beings that consist of stardust and are still a physical part of the universe, be unrelated to it? The idea is not only absurd, but it is also psychologically worrying, since it denies our basic oneness with nature. It is the same idea that ignores the oneness with our environment on Earth and that gives us the right to abuse and destroy it. It is polarity stuck in either/or. If common sense is applied, the existence of life and of humanity inside the universe has to be seen as inseparably interwoven. Every detail we can observe in the cosmos proves this fact:

The size of the universe for example is given by multiplying the age by the speed of light, which equals 10^{10} years. Man requires carbon for life. Carbon is generated in the stars; supernova explosions scatter carbon through space. This can only happen after nuclear burning.

Nuclear burning takes more than 10^{10} years. Therefore, the size of the universe is a prerequisite for carbon (on our scale) and humans (on our scale) to exist. Practically none of the necessary conditions for humans to exist can be explained by a random evolution! The universe has to be extremely finely tuned to these constants allowing our existence.

For human metabolism to work, there has to be a certain temperature. Too high a temperature will degrade the enzymes, and too low a temperature will halt the chemical reactions and life will end. The suitable temperature has to be close to the energy of molecular interaction. Then there are three states of matter in the human body, the solid and the liquid states, and a human must also breathe gas. Therefore, the Earth must have an atmosphere at a temperature of about 100 degrees K. This requirement places a constraint on the Earth's mass. It cannot be too small, since bodies with small mass have small velocities of escape, gas would not be retained—and would escape into space. Also, the gravitation constant G has to be very precisely tuned to allow for human life. For humankind to evolve, we require the sun to be well settled in the main sequence stage for several billion years or more. This requirement makes us realize that G must not be too large or too small. It can only take the observed value. If G is too large, then the sun would have soon evolved into the high temperature stage and would not have been able to remain in the main sequence for some billions of years. If G is too small, then it would be impossible for the sun to reach the main sequence stage, and the sun would be lingering about in the low temperature stage. Thus, only when G takes the present known value—will the solar system be maintained long enough in a condition favourable to the ascent of humankind. Another point is that the process of element synthesis depends heavily on the weak interacting constant gw. If gw is too large, then neutron decay would be faster, and neutrons would have disappeared through decay at the start of nucleo-synthesis. Such a universe only has protons and no neutrons. No heavy elements can form, nor can humankind. On the other hand, if gw is too small, then the number ratio between neutrons and protons would have 'frozen out' at a very early cosmic time, when the temperature was very high. The result would be a hydrogen-less universe, and once again it would be impossible for the human race to evolve. Therefore, in order to provide various chemical elements that humans require, gw must have taken roughly its present value.

Practically all other constants we find in the universe are similarly related to the very narrow specifications of human existence. These extraordinary 'coincidences' prove beyond any doubt the relatedness between the human existence and the physical universe. But they do themselves not provide positive evidence for the universe being the physical germ of the human form, since fish, chicken and apes are just as related to the narrow specifications of the same universe! Also, the form of the universe, one might argue, could be a completely unknown form altogether. However, if the universal form were entirely different from every-thing we know to be part of it, the laws of repetition of form hierarchically and the principle of connectedness and many other rules of nature would be broken! Only if the universal form is a repetition of known forms, does it make any sense having the parts it contains. Undeniable fact is that this universe contains not only the building blocks and conditions for life, but that it contains life itself! This is the most important quality of the universe and has to be considered as a foremost principle of its functions.

If a part of a system is a living organism, there is no way that the system as a whole could be less alive! The question therefore has to be—which of the known living forms can account for the universal form and—does the universe give us a clue, whether it should be a tree, or a chicken, or a monkey, or a form beyond our imagination? And to sharpen the question—what 'germ' can we detect at our level of the hierarchy that 'knows' exactly how to evolve to the final size of the universal form?

A clue to this exists indeed, and it is far more than just a clue:

The human consciousness is such a system which relates more than any-thing to the universal form! It is a system of quantum processes capable of asking questions like—what is the form of the universe?

In order to ask such a question, the quantum processes in the brain have to tune precisely into the large, physical realities of the universe, and for every image we have of a galaxy or an apple, there must be the microcosmic equivalent in our brain, which is an exact copy of the 'real' macro-cosmic form. Only the human consciousness (of every known system), does hence relate to the universal form in a hierarchically symmetrical and functional way!

We are therefore not relying on assumptions or speculations when we consider the candidates for the form that includes all other forms. We can actually come to a precise and scientifically sound conclusion if we consider the properties the universe must have, in order for it to be as it is. The universal form has to account for all other forms in existence in physically quantifiable terms and as the blueprint design. If the universal form were, say a tree, it would not account for the existence of the chicken in the same universe, since the form of a chicken is not genetically or otherwise contained in the seed (genes, consciousness) of a tree. The universal form has to 'know' the blue-print for all its composite parts, and all forms have to be represented by the universal form. Which forms on Earth, must we ask, contain any other forms of life, either directly or as a code—ready to be translated into the physical reality of expansion? Surely, the chicken can host a few micro-organisms within its physical integrity and so does the tree. The chicken may even account for the tree, if it sees or eats its seeds, and so assimilates the tree's genes. But how does the egg of a chicken account for the elephant, the coconut and the motorcar? How can all of these forms be contained in a chicken that would then account for them all? The answer to this riddle flows directly from the hierarchical mechanics of form, which can reproduce itself genetically, (but also in other hierarchical ways). For example, if we look at an apple and then close our eyes, we can still 'see' the form of the apple. Physically speaking, the form of the apple has reproduced itself via contraction, by the code of light, and then, when it reaches the projecting plane of our mind, rearranged itself (as the original form) on a still chemical, but now microcosmic level of morphic manifestation. We are of course used to consider sense-experience as the perception of an objective and unalterable reality where we, the observer, are separate from the observed objects. Only the advent of quantum physics has hinted at a reality where the very act of observation alters the observed object.

In truth, we are however just as much the 'victim' of such an act of observation as we are the manipulator! Form travels by the means of light, and uses our consciousness as a plane for projection on which it can reproduce itself on a quantum level. For every apple we observe, this same apple is chemically reproduced in our mind, in order to form the image we can then see. The physical existence of this new (remembered) apple is as real as that of the original, only it has fluctuated into its minimum point of contraction, where it closely resembles its genetic structure. The difference between the reproduction of the apple by projecting its form onto the microcosmic plane of the genes on one hand—and its reproduction by projection onto the quantum reality of the observing mind on the other—is minimal, if at all existent. In both cases, the apple is fully preserved, as far as its identity of form is concerned, and in both cases, it has the potential for a new manifestation on its maximum point of expansion!

How many apples have been drawn, sculpted and recreated from various materials—and thereby had their form contracted onto the micro-cosmic level of the human mind, before expanding that form again onto its maximum point? The creative or reproductive urge of the human mind is an inescapable consequence of the mechanics of forms stored within the brain to move from microcosmic existence back towards maximum manifestation. Consciousness hereby 'obeys' the mechanics of form that urges it to 'recreate' the original form. This is also how we create our accidents and how we make our dreams come true. The cause of all creation is thus prescribed in detail by the mechanics of the universal form!

Certainly, at this stage of our evolution the recreation of the universal form is still incomplete, and a wooden or plastic apple cannot have a form identical to the original apple. However, we cannot equate our present stage of human consciousness with the consciousness of mature humanity at the end of universal growth! In millions of years from now, humanity may not only perceive an apple visually, but be conscious of its entire structure, and therefore capable to reproduce it accurately by its quantum mechanical processes of thought. At our present stage, we may not be able to reconstruct every form we are conscious of yet, but we are already capable to visualize all the forms we know in our semi-conscious mind. We can see the form of a chicken even when there is no physical presence, and we see the form of an elephant, and the form of a motorcar. All these images are chemical realities in our brain and have the potential to be reproduced once again. That is why we go to the zoo—to restore the maximum of our mental images! We cannot avoid following the dictates of form—as all known forms are structured into the conscious and subconscious human mind. The entire history of humankind is an example of increasing perfection in our attempt to reproduce forms. The invention of the aeroplane is nothing but an attempt to reproduce the form of birds as it is perceived by our senses and contracted into our mind. The invention of the electric light-bulb is an imitation of the Sun and of the stars, and the motorcar could only be 'invented,' when it was perceived that the wheels in the sky were related to motion. It could not have been created before such a notion was present in the mind.

Every single invention is a combination of preexistent forms as contained in our consciousness and nothing truly original can ever be created therefore. Our scientific progress is not random at all, but follows the patterns given by the forms that are already contained in the human mind. This is why knowledge cannot be taught, as Plato strongly emphasized—but only 'recollected.' The reason why there is a conscious mind and also a subconscious mind is that the movement of mental evolution runs from a pool containing all preexistent forms in the universe to their gradual actualization on the maximum side of their existence. The greatest insight science can achieve at this stage is to recognize the human mind as a complete microcosm that contains all forms, either subconsciously or consciously, in their physical and chemical, but always microcosmic manifestations. In an evolving consciousness, the 'images' of form continue to achieve structural detail and precision and will eventually be reproduced on their maximum scale as they move towards their opposites. Even if these quantum mechanical reproductions of form in our brains cannot yet be mathematically quantified, nobody can doubt their existence. How else could a plastic apple ever be made—if the blue-print of the form apple did not exist within the mind of the creator?

If we understand this, the riddle of the Cosmic Egg is solved: Only the human form of all forms in the known universe is capable to account for all other forms—since consciousness of form is the existence of form on the microcosmic level! The universe therefore needs to have a 'human observer' who is the universal minimum that can fathom its own maximum. It has to be at least a human cell, in order to genetically contain the potential consciousness of every form in this universe!

The chicken in this universe, as all other forms, can only evolve because it has originally been a virtual, conscious or subconscious reality in the genetic program of the quark, from the beginning. And it really only had to exist as a visual experience in the consciousness of a previous generation of cosmic humanity in order to make a new morphogenetic appearance in this cycle! In terms of the cosmic egg, the chicken, together with all other forms, is part of the 'common subconscious' which existed from the time when this universe was conceived. This common subconscious, which all of humanity shares, therefore contains what Jung called the 'archetypal forms,' which are preexistent forms. It summarizes every form the last generation of mature human form has been conscious of, at the time of 'conception.' Apart from all known forms preexisting this particular universe, they have also been a part of the human mind since the 'Big Bang!'

We were once a tree, a fish, a lizard, a bird—and all those steps of human 'evolution' mean that these forms are now a permanent part of the human psyche and of the human DNA! Even the elephant is a branch of human awareness. Man is thus not one of many unrelated forms—but contains all other forms historically, and fundamentally, in his collective psyche!

One could of course argue, that any other existent conscious species in this universe, beside the human form, might claim the same quality of consciousness. Empirically, such a conscious non-humanoid form does not exist in this universe, despite our misplaced humility of no longer thinking ourselves special any longer. The simple truth is, that there can be no tiny chicken-observer in an elephant-universe!

Besides, a random evolution of intelligent forms in this universe would have produced several more advanced beings, capable, and some of them willing, to influence humanity and to make themselves very known. Some of them would have been around for millions of years. This is however not so, simply because we don't live in a universe that knows any intelligent, space-travelling, non-humanoid life-forms, no matter how hard the film directors try to come up with non-humanoid aliens. The cosmic egg argument provides precisely the conditions for a

Human Embryo to exist and develop, and we find, as soon as we start learning how to look in more circumspect ways, that every detail in the entire universe is designed to precisely fit our human conditions.

Humans did not only evolve from the universe, but the universe itself evolved from the human form—another 'paradox' of opposite truths!

The existence of human consciousness in itself provides overwhelming evidence that all existence in this universe can be traced back to that singularity of form which can comprehend this universe, that contains the design, the microcosmic blue-print, of all its manifestations. The human form is hence, in compliance with the principles of quantum mechanics and the mechanics of form, the only possible form that can account for the precise structure and nature of this universe.

There is no observer inside a non-living universe!

The 'morphological germ' inside any form is the only thing capable of asking what his universe is, can be, or will be!

19. Oneness and the Cosmic Mother

When so many new physical principles and physical fields have been introduced in order to account for the properties of atoms and sub-atomic particles, the conventional assumption that no new physical principles or fields come into play at levels of organization above the atom seems remarkably arbitrary. Every cosmological theory so far has failed to describe the genesis of the universe as a whole in a way that accounts for its complexity of forms, for the laws of nature, and for the existence of conscious life. Chemical evolution and selective process can only explain how a certain form develops, but the design of this form in the first place is not in principle describable or predictable in mechanistic terms. How does the stardust 'know' the form of a chicken into which it assembles? Genetic determination only works for chicken that come after the first chicken. But how does the first chicken come into existence, or how does evolution know the design towards which the chicken has to develop? How can the paradox be solved of whether there first was the chicken or its egg?

The hypothesis of formative causation is only concerned with the repetition of form and not with its appearance in the first place. It has therefore never been applied in the context of cosmogony or in the context of first appearance of form in this universe. However, according to the Cosmic Egg Theory, the morphogenesis in and of the universe is not a 'first move' but a repetition of form. The theory of formative causation is however still a helpful bridge between conventional physical theory and the Cosmic Egg. There may not be a need to resort to the influence of eternal archetypal forms or transcendent mathematical truths, if form itself creates the hierarchical continuum. The form of the chicken needs to be but preexistent on a higher level of the hierarchy in order for the stardust in our universe to be ordered by this higher 'field' of previous existence, and assembled by the means of 'evolution' —until it becomes an egg, and a chicken again, on a new level of existence. The question of whether there first was the egg or the chicken cannot be answered from within our linear mind-set for the simple reason that evolution is not a linear or unique process, but a continuum of hierarchical repetitions without an absolute beginning. Logically, there are only the alternatives of either to artificially assign the 'first move' to an archetypal form—or to see the continuum of form as non-causal and unlimited. Generations of universes following each other. 'Evolution,' within our range of awareness, can only be the reproductive processes of chemicals and virtual forms developing towards their maximum, their manifestation on a larger level.

The difference between evolution and genetic reproduction is thus only the difference between an observer contemplating the reproduction of form from inside or from outside the form.

During morphogenesis on all levels of existence the higher level 'field' modifies the probability of probabilistic events in the lower-level morphic units under its influence exactly as a parent influences the form of his off-spring via the genes. Hence, the universe as a whole is clearly the 'morphogenetic field' ordering the 'big bang' and the appearance of all known forms within the new morphogenetic germ.

Evolution is thus given the direction and the design as required for probabilistic events to lead to unique forms as we know them, and as we will truly know them when they are finalized. The larger morphogenetic field ordering the 'first move' of this universe, and responsible for all its forms, can be recognized by the forms it produces. Since the universe contains living organisms and consciousness, the morphogenetic field ordering it has to be a living organism and conscious of all there can be. It must be at least as complex and intelligent as are the composite parts of its morphogenetic germ. It must therefore be at least as complex and intelligent as humankind as a whole! If the higher-level field containing this universe were any-thing but the human form, there could be no accounting for human consciousness, since the field would have to be less complex than the parts of its germ. Besides, the fact that the universe is comprehensible to humans, but not to other forms, shows the symmetrical genetic relationship between the universe and the human mind too clearly to arrive at any other conclusion. Only the human form includes all other forms in the universe by the microcosmic process of conscious and subconscious thought. The human mind is the microcosmic mirror of universal reality and has the ability to reproduce the cosmic complexity by understanding. It seems, that we are indeed made in 'God's image' and that the human form simply is the only form capable to fit its consciousness to the physical realities of this particular universe—like a lock and key. However, the mature human form which preceded our universe does not compare very much with the human form on the evolutionary stage of our time. It is rather the end-result of what to us is a complete evolution of our universe, and resembles more the human form as it will be in billions of years from now. It cannot even be taken for granted that the human form at the end of its evolution will still be dependent on any physical manifestations. The human form may develop towards pure consciousness, pure form, without the need for a body, but retaining the ability to materialize and to manifest form. All we can know for certain is that the cosmic human form has at some stage before the big bang taken on the form we today consider as human.

Metaphysically, the mature human form on the super-cosmic level may not quite fit our ideas of the human form as we know it, but in a few billion years of time may fit every definition of what we commonly call 'God!' It may be difficult to accept this ultimate position of the human form at a time when we have just learned to refute human relevance in a universal context. But only a short time ago (in evolutionary terms), humankind did very much see itself as the 'crown of creation' at the centre of the universe, and felt a holy respect for the human role in creation.

Strangely, native societies throughout history believed in a Mother Goddess, the Earth Mother who brought forth all life, from planets to animals to human beings to the stars in the sky. The ancient, pagan religions now prove to have been scientifically correct all along! The idea of a Cosmic Mother who gives birth to all life in the universe fits perfectly with existing scientific facts and provides the missing puzzle-pieces of genesis and of the human condition. The Cosmic Mother is the Oneness from which the complexity of our universe has emerged and only She provides a system capable of explaining the hierarchical continuity of nature in a unifying way. The Cosmic Mother keeps a mechanical God of First Creation out of our immediate physical universe and moves the transcendental question further back into the realms of infinity. The scope of science and particularly of cosmology becomes wide open again, like so many times before in the history of human thought. At a time when we think our most primitive ignorance shed for good, and when most mysteries seem explained in principle, yet another fundamental miracle is discovered, and our own limited perception once more faced, in order for humankind to proceed with growing towards final maturity.

The Mother fits all theoretical systems including legends and religions perfectly, like no other concept ever did. Even the biblical word of genesis—God created human beings 'in his image' can be taken literally, apart from the implied exclusively male aspect. The Cosmic Egg is used as a symbol of Creation in India, Indonesia, in Japan, Greece, by the Baltic people, in Africa and by the red Indians of the Americas. The Celts, who were admired by Socrates, Aristotle and Plato as the wisest people on Earth for their druidic knowledge, and who built the sophisticated astronomical computer of Stonehenge, worshiped the Cosmic Egg as their symbol for the origin of life and divine fertility in creation. On the Hawaiian Islands, genesis was managed by a team of spirits skilled in embryology and child development. And the ancient Chinese, who knew so much then, of what western cosmology has just recently begun to discover, spelled it our quite clearly: 'The universe is an egg, and Pan Gu is born there-in!' There are also numerous reports of visions various people have had about a 'cosmic' woman, either in dreams or in states of altered consciousness. The countless appearances of a woman 'floating' or 'hovering' in the air, as reported by crowds of assembled people, were often understood to be appearances of the virgin Mary, since this is the likely interpretation for Christian observers. But if religious interpretations are stripped off pure observation—what remains is the image of a 'supernatural' woman hovering in the sky. A Hindu crowd would, under the same circumstances as given in Lourdes, have seen Sita or Parvati. If we trust that so many people did not all have the same hallucination, we have to accept that either a human female was in fact perceived hovering above the ground, or at least that the image of a human female form-field was 'received.' Since a visual projection by technological means was not yet possible at the time, this 'field' had to be a natural phenomenon. Therefore, apart from assuming a female with antigravity abilities or alien technology, we have to arrive at the conclusion that a 'morphogenetic field,' or a vision of a human female from an unknown dimension had been 'received.' If the reported verbal communication factually came from this female form, the field must have been created, directed and employed for a purpose. If we accept these appearances of a human female, (which have been confirmed by research), advising and admonishing from a higher realm, it would not seem so strange that the onlookers identified Her as the 'Mother of God,' who to Christians can only be the virgin Mary. The morphogenetic 'field,' given by genetics, of the cosmic Mother sheds light on all these verified appearances, and can explain them as transmissions from a higher hierarchical reality, without disturbing the mystical quality of the experience. There is indeed no theoretical approach to the origin and the nature of Creation that can substitute for the existence of the Cosmic Mother and of Creation without creating more unsolvable paradox and more questions. If for example the universe were proposed to be something like pure thought, or a brain wave, the consequence would be the question of who is the thinker of this thought, which brings us back onto the right path.

The Mother and Son answer the question of whether God is male or female in an as-well-as answer, where the Mother is the hyperbolic, previous, contemporary, and surrounding universe that holds the new universe.

A complete truth has to have unifying character, which means that no specific religion can be favoured over others, and no old dogma can remain unchallenged. A metaphysical truth must be consistent with the realities of the physical world and with scientific fact. The contradictions between scientific theory and religious belief throughout history were clear indications for the limitedness of their scope. The Cosmic Egg Theory is the only possible system of absolutely universal character and reunites fact with mystery, and science with ancient intuition—and all the paradoxes of logical thought with the simplicity of Oneness. The supreme virtue of the theory is however the perfect symmetry and beauty with which it reconciles the creation of the physical universe with the existence of the human form.

20. The Growing Egg

In a sense, the universe started from nothing.

Before the Cosmic Egg started to grow, it did not exist. However, what cosmogonists explain with a vacuum fluctuation did not happen in a vacuum but in the ovaries of the Cosmic Mother and proceeded what we describe as meiosis in biology. Long before the 'big bang,' the new universe began to be prepared with the development of oogania. The particles that pass down the form of the parent organism onto the microscopic level of the genes are the same particles that convey the preexistent universal form to that first nucleon which marks the beginning of universal expansion. These particles convey the design of the parental form and translate it into a 'virtual form' on a much smaller hierarchical level. To the observer on the genetic level of form it seems as if the resulting 'germ' appears out of nowhere. The new copy can naturally never be recognized as such, but gives the impression of having been originally created from nothing.

Far from resembling a fiery explosion, the young cell then consisted mainly of water, or else of galaxies with large hydrogen molecules. At this stage, it already contained the principle of 'virtual life,' but the genes, we might call them the 'sleepers,' could not yet awaken to actual life and were unable to change or to move into a direction. Humankind as we know it, did then not exist as a living physical reality, but only as a virtual potential for life and as the physical building-block that held half of the necessary design. The human genetic potential derived from the singularity of parental form was contracted into the micro-space of the genes, but suspended from realization. But how, must we ask, does this early aqueous universe compare with a fire-ball of expanding matter and energy, as required for the fusion of atomic nuclei?

How can fire evolve in water, when fire and water are such incompatible opposites?

The conventional conception has always held, that fire and water limit and threaten each others existence and cannot possibly coexist. This idea is however very wrong! In truth, the elements create each other in a causal cycle and can only be understood as totally interdependent, and as aspects of each other and of the principle of life. To understand this, we have to examine the chronological 'evolution' of these two elements in the history of our own planet: First, there was only fire, and the whole planet was so hot that no other element could exist. However, the other elements were already potentially contained in the glowing lava, and when the high temperature eventually cooled, the elements of Earth, air and water could gradually evolve from implicit potentialities. The key question is now, from what preexisting element the element of fire evolved if it did not come into existence from nowhere! Air and wood are only fuel, but not the source of fire, and cannot explain its genesis. Again, we can best learn from the parts of nature we already know, and we just have to ask how fire is produced in the observable environment.

Fire can be found naturally in the shape of lightening, which originates from friction between rain-clouds, which consist of water molecules. Another genesis of heat can be observed at the bottom of a compost heap, where it is also produced by humidity. Even in the human body, fire in the form of body-heat is maintained in an aqueous solution, by the process of metabolism. The hydrogen bomb is a man-made example for the creation of fire from the quint-essential property of water—hydrogen. As a matter of fact, the main fuel for all the stars in the universe is hydrogen, which is also the element that preexisted all other elements. This has already been realized by early Greek philosophy which held that the heavenly bodies were ignited clouds! Noticing, that fire arises from water, we can answer the question of what element preceded the fire of the early universe. The answer is, that in the beginning every-thing had to be water, and that fire was born from water! The reason why this is not common knowledge is again the hierarchical organization of nature: When fire arises from water, we cannot see actual flames, because fire exists latently on the microcosmic level of the water molecules.

If one imagines observing from a scale where water molecules appear as galaxies, the behaviour of water changes dramatically. Instead of reminding of the liquid state, it consists of vast empty spaces and star-like bodies at large distances from each other. From this position, it becomes clear to the observer how fire can exist in the micro-space of water, without the apparent problem of its immediate termination by the liquid state! Exactly the same situation exists in our own bodies where fire coexists with water on a microcosmic level and thereby keeps us warm, active and alive. Life always develops from water as the primary element, be it the first micro-organisms on Earth that certainly evolved in water—or the baby developing for nine months in the waters of her mother—or the aqueous life-processes we daily maintain—or the birth of the universe as a cell consisting of water.

Given that the genesis of fire so obviously requires the presence of water, it is surprising that modern cosmogonists have never asked the question of how the fire of the big bang came into being as an element! To the logic-loving Greeks however, Creation was elemental, and Thales of Miletus knew then that the universe originally was water! Surely the principles of elemental genesis as observed on Earth cannot be valid on one level of scale and invalid on another. If we can observe fire to exist on the micro-level of water every-where in nature, we simply cannot help but conclude that the early universe had to consist of water on a large scale. The fire of the 'big bang' evolved in the microcosmic space of water molecules, which is the level we are able to observe.

At the time of the first oogania, the element of fire was already present, and it could of course be identified as a cause for the universal growth, from an energetic point of view. The existence of fire in the early, aqueous universe is consistent with the existence of life in the universal cell, since it is indicative of metabolic processes. The great temperatures in the young universe were produced by the micro-processes called catabolism, which means a breaking down of molecules (the size of galaxies) for fuel. The temperatures, as measured from the planetary scale of humanity, were so tremendous, that they could fuse the stars and galaxies of our perspective into completely different structures, as required by the needs of the cosmic cellular metabolism. This is how the fusion of the heavy atomic nuclei occurred. However, not all nuclei were fused from the substances already contained in the cell. Other materials from outside the egg provided an inflow of nutrients that then had to be assimilated by the processes of catabolism. The relative heat of these micro-processes will prove to account for the high temperatures of the early universe, if related to the hierarchical scale from which we observe. From the time when the oogania were formed, the growth-rate became slower and more constant, which is exactly what cosmology describes to have happened to the expansion of the young universe. During oogenesis the leptotene became zygotene, pachitene,diplotene and finally a primordial follicle. The oocyte-growth was reduced to a 100-400-fold increase in cell volume. Later, during what we call meiosis, the diploid nucleus divided twice, producing a total of four nuclei. At this stage, the duality in the young cell became non-dualistic again, thus losing the ability to approach its future form momentarily. The symmetries of the haploid nuclei became more perfect again, but produced the sterility of an unfertilized egg. The chromosomes replicated only once—prior to the first nuclear division. We know that in human females, the meiotic divisions produce haploid nuclei, but the cytoplasm is apportioned unequally during cytokinesis in both meiosis I and II.

The cosmic egg was therefore produced along with two or three polar bodies! These polar bodies contain the other post-meiotic nuclei, and usually disintegrate after a while.

Cosmology cannot directly deduce that the universe has divided since it started to expand, because from within the cell such a division cannot be observed. A cell-division does not influence the structure of the new cells, nor does it leave any trace that could be detected by the means of astronomy. However, there are indications of missing matter in cosmology that point directly at those polar bodies that coexist or coexisted for a time—outside of the universe! The reason, why this 'dark matter' is only gravitationally detectable, without being luminous, can be found in its position beyond the cell-membrane of this universe, which is impenetrable to light. No more than three such dark universes should therefore be detectable. Knowing the mass of polar bodies, relative to the ovum, it should be possible to confirm their existence by testing their relative gravitational strength. Some of the 'broken symmetries' in this universe could be accounted for by the breaking up of the primary oocyte into an ovum and three polar bodies.

When the ovum was fully evolved, the principle of life in the universe was still suspended and the 'sleepers' were lingering in a haploid state of 'virtual life.' Around this time finally happened what we today may call the event of genesis—the fertilization of the fully mature ovum—aptly called the 'Big Bang'. What biology mechanistically describes as a fusion of male and female cells and the pairing of genes, would have been quite a spectacular event, if experienced from within the ovum! Nothing less than the 'incarnation' of spirited life and of a potential human mind, capable of becoming conscious of God, happened with the act of fertilization! The inrush of life must have been accompanied by physical phenomena of extraordinary proportions and it would be well beyond all biological, physical, and philosophical imagination to describe this and any (relative) beginning of a human soul from the quantum level. What we may call the 'Big Bang' was the beginning of growth in all directions, of actual purpose, and definitely of a fundamentally new physical situation on the quantum level of the cosmic egg. Nothing short of a miracle, this event created some-thing from nothing as it would seem—if only this physical universe is considered as real. Resisting the temptation to philosophize on this 'nothing' or 'nowhere', we can only state in biological terms that two preexistent singular units of 'virtual life' fused into a single diploid ovum, which then suddenly was in a state of 'evolution' and on its way to become conscious! The two haploid gametes fused to a single, diploid cell, which then contained symmetrical pairs of chromosomes. Physically, this is the reason why the universe contains so many symmetrical pairs that did not exist before the cosmic egg was fertilized. The fertilized ovum then came under the full influence of the 'morphogenetic field' of its parental form, and the genes started to determine the programmed development of the universe. The universal expansion was now related by the genes—and all the physical (and biological) forces in the ovum were ordered by the design the genes had contracted from the previous form. Only a little time later (about 10 billion of our years), the egg evolved to the stage, where on its quantum level it started to produce physical manifestations of its germ. The beginning of life on Earth marks the beginning of foetal growth as observed from the micro-space within the egg. Structures started to become more pronounced as the organelles worked to sustain the process of evolution. The bigger the universe grew, the cooler it seemed to become. Even the warmth from outside the universe would seem reduced if measured from within the growing cell. But on the cosmic scale warmth is maintained evenly. Its equal distribution can be deduced from observations of the cosmic background radiation, which seems to be the radiation of warmth emanating from the maternal body. The core of the universe was even at this stage not the vacuum it would be if an explosion had catapulted all matter and energy from their point of origin, but it was dense, like the cores of stars and galaxies are denser than the rest of their mass. It might be futile for us today to look for the core of the universe, as it is futile for fish to try and find water, since we live in the middle of it all. But a possible way for testing could be to measure the density of galactic distribution at large distances. Improved telescopes might reveal an abruptly reduced spatial density outside a definite radius from the centre of the universe, when compared to inside of this radius. The existence of other organelles, like the mitochondria or the cytoskeleton, could also be proven if we analyse the evidence of 'dark matter' inside the universe. Since organelles have a membrane just like the cell itself—there have to be seemingly non-luminous clusters of large size in this universe, which will not easily reveal their identity, since light does not penetrate the membranes.

It is also difficult to observe the cell-divisions of the universe—but cosmology has noticed a gradual slowing down of the universal expansion rate! The mechanistic deduction that the universe is eventually going to collapse is based on this observation. The Cosmic Egg Theory however can explain the 'braking effect' not with the galaxies' gravitational tug on one another, which is only a secondary cause—but with the preparation of the growing cosmic cell for its next cellular division.

Cell-division has probably already happened during cosmic meiosis, and it is going to happen again. Before a cell divides, its growth-rate decelerates and eventually stops until the division is complete. Omega is indeed equal to one, since the cell is in an equilibrium between the expanding forces and the contracting forces. But this does not affect the cellular growth rate. The conclusion that a decelerating universe is either going to decelerate forever, or collapse, is unfounded, because the growth of the universe is not determined but only conducted by the physical forces. In a cellular universe, the deceleration of growth is a normal phenomenon before every division and does not contradict any of the physical laws governing the cell. The deceleration of universal expansion only demonstrates once again, that the universe is not a machine and that it therefore does not have a constant expansion rate at all times. The prediction of further cell-divisions is backed by the evidence of omnipresent symmetrical pairs of physical phenomena, which is a requirement for cell-divisions. Each new cell needs its own copy of a nucleus and its own chromosome pairs, and these copies have to be produced prior to every division. Since the copies of form, like all reproduction of form, have to be organized from the quantum level upwards, we will find perfectly symmetrical building-blocks of matter even on our planetary scale. The contemporary universe evinces many perfectly symmetrical pairs of particles, while all the original symmetries given by the mechanics of form ought to be 'broken' by the expansion of the universe, which is the movement away from its point of original symmetry.

The 'broken' symmetries of today are the symmetries between the 'morphogenetic field' and the 'morphogenetic germ,' and are restored only when the oscillating universal form reaches the maximum point of expansion. But the 'perfect symmetries' of today are possibly indications for a future cell-division that requires an organization of exact copies for the new cell.

In the universe of our time, all the enigmas and paradoxes resulting from the mechanistic view can be demonstrated to be natural phenomena as encountered in a fertilized ovum!

The boundedness of the universe for example is given by the definite size of the ovum at any stage of its growth, and finally by the mature size of the cosmic human form. But in the wider context of hierarchical continuity, the ovum is resting within a larger womb-structure that surrounds it, and has a curvature tending towards the hyperbolic, which reconciles the paradox of rounded/hyperbolic. The Celts symbolized this phenomenon by the female vessel containing an egg.

The boundedness of the egg is in no way contradictory to the even larger hierarchical spaces of cosmic existence, which still may stretch towards infinity. Thus can finiteness and infinity coexist without posing a metaphysical problem. The creation of something from nothing is similarly self-evident, as already demonstrated, and the ultimate paradox of the 'creation' of life from 'no-life' can only be solved by the mechanics of form. The existing concepts of closed/open, bounded/unbounded, limited/unlimited, or spherical/hyperbolic are all incorrect where they try to decide for either/or! These paradoxes do only exist within the mechanistic model, but disappear when seen in the light of the living universe. All these 'strange' phenomena like 'missing matter,' 'black holes,' 'local groups,' the decelerating universe, or any other phenomenon in our universe, are not unexplainable and disconnected coincidences within a random evolution, but make perfect sense within the system of an ovum, and could not be thought away without destroying the functional identity of the growing egg. What is so vaguely described as a vacuum fluctuation can physically only be understood as a fluctuation of form, which via a quantum jump of genetic contraction produces the ooganium from a dimension that to the observer positioned inside the cell—must appear as 'nowhere.' The only model that can possibly account for genesis and all the discussed phenomena of this universe is the Cosmic Egg, since what we experience as the universe today is a system which is exquisitely tuned to the requirements of the growing human existence. It perfectly relates and conforms to what is comprehensible to the human mind, and it reveals the most powerful factor in human psychology—the love between mother and child—as the ultimate physical reality! Like the koans of Zen-buddhism, the paradoxes of the universe show the path to Oneness, and have led us to the meeting-point of mind and matter, which is the human consciousness of Self.

21.The Embryo

The most characteristic property of a fertilized ovum is that it contains the germ of a new living being. If the genes in an ovum are human genes, the ovum must be a human ovum. One of the most powerful arguments for the Cosmic Egg is therefore the existence of human beings in this universe. One will ask how humankind as we know it compares with the existence of a human embryo on a cosmic scale—especially since humans inhabit only a single planet which in a cosmological context seems too insignificant in size to count quantitatively. To give some perspective to our relative scale within the fertilized Egg, it can be estimated that the star cluster of which the Milky Way is a part corresponds to a strand of DNA on a single Chromosome of the cosmic ovum. Humankind as a whole provides the complete set of information on the DNA-ladder of this chromosome, and each individual human being contributes a small set of information towards the whole. Part of the information held by an individual is genetically passed down from previous generations, but the experience gathered during a life-cycle also becomes part of the genetic pool that we then pass on to the next generation, and ultimately to the genetic pool of the Cosmic Embryo. The fusion of ovum and sperm brings about the need for change, and for new combinations in order to produce a unique new being. These changes and re-combinations are thus the essence of what humankind experiences as life, as learning, and as individual development. Proposing several billions of human beings to become a single embryo is really no different from the idea of billions of bytes of information constituting the genes of a single organism. We may feel reduced by this analogy, but in a technical sense the human brain is indeed a computer holding information that can be passed on by communication, or creativity, or reproduction. Life is inseparably linked to the fate of genetic information contained by the ovum.

As far as physical survival is concerned, every cell and every part of it will eventually disintegrate, and therefore a human being also has to die. However, the genetic information and experience once collected does not die with the death of a physical gene, but survives the cycle of life and death! It gets passed on to new generations or new 'incarnations' of genetic substance that will then contain a precise copy of this information. It is however not each single experience that can survive genetically, since this would require an ever-growing genetic data-bank. Only the essence of what has been improved can be preserved genetically. Therefore, when we die, all the repetitious details of our life-experience are lost. This is exactly how the Asian concept of 'karma' describes reincarnation, where the circumstances of every new life-time are built on the achievements of the previous life. The new physical carrier of the preserved information will regularly not remember his identity in a previous life, but he is still essentially the same individual. The genetic mechanics thus allow for a preservation of the individual identity of human beings within the continuum of form!

The mystical concepts of 'karma' and 'reincarnation' are obviously compatible with the mechanics of genes, and also the Christian concept of a 'Heaven' hints at an afterlife for the individual human experience on a higher and united platform. Another strong confirmation for humankind being linked to a single unit is Jung's theory of the common unconscious. Humans may see a wide variance in the unique information they each represent, but subconsciously there are still major identical structures that every-one shares. Several theories have therefore suggested that humankind is one united family with a common destiny or a 'super-soul!'

The major religions see humankind as one entity (of sisters and brothers) that has to become aware of its basic Oneness. Even in ancient Greece we find the notion that identifies the world intellect with God.

Thales held there was a divine mind which formed all things out of water, and that all things had a soul. Ultimately he believed in 'innumerable worlds,' which make up a 'boundless body!'

Political and social efforts have the ultimate goal of uniting humankind, and evolution itself demonstrates that we are well on our way to the same goal. Evolution shows that physical differences between the races, and also between the sexes and individuals, tend to disappear gradually, while the human mind takes over more and more of our physical functions. It is not difficult to predict that evolution aims for a growing and united consciousness, while the physical body will be needed less and less and may finally even be replaced by the faculties of the mind. Ultimately, the human evolution is moving towards a form characterized less by its physical manifestation than by the structure of its consciousness. It would therefore be plausible to predict that humankind after millions of years of evolution will have fused to a single united consciousness!

The rapidly growing technologies of communication in our time show how this is achieved by linking the parts into a network of One that then contains the experience of all participants. If we consider the principal psychological factors in human behaviour, our evolution towards Oneness becomes even more obvious: All the characteristics typical of the human mind, like the drive to learn, the need for competition, improvement and self-knowledge, and of course our greatest mystery of all—the existence of love—show this evolution to move towards a higher platform of united Self. Certainly, our consciousness of Oneness at this point in time is only at the very beginning of its evolution, and we should not expect to achieve the ultimate goal collectively within the next few years, even if this is possible for individuals. Our bodies have really just emerged from the substance of the Earth and our mind still emphasizes the comforts of matter and body more than it seeks the spirit in nature, music or art. Most people still cannot envision a future beyond their own life-span, and are overwhelmed by the threat of their own permanent destruction—because they are still trapped by the fear over their limited physical existence. In a spiritual sense, we may still remain the unborn embryo for a very long time yet, and even the mere idea of humankind as one single organism still threaten our narrow descriptions of life just as Galileo's concepts threatened the scientific explanations of his contemporaries. But the challenges to our world views are going further yet:

The Cosmic Embryo does not only consist of humanity on the planet Earth alone! The human seed is spread out in this universe and has evolved to a similar stage on as many planets as there are chromosomes in the Cosmic Egg.

The existence of humanoid extra-terrestrial intelligence, as proposed by legend, fairy-tale, biblical descriptions, and fantasy (which are reproductions of subconscious forms) cannot all be without substance. The angels of the Old Testament on their 'fiery chariots,' the Greek Gods of 'supernatural powers,' and all the many 'Gods' that appeared to practically every ancient culture, had in common that they were all humanoid in form! There are rock-carvings in South and Central America, describing Gods arriving from other star-systems with star-ships, and there are a great many similar reports confirming such events in most cultures. The reason why our galaxy seems devoid of extra-terrestrial intelligence lies in the vast distances given by the genes in separate chromosome clusters. But in accordance with the network of information in genes, which needs to be physically conveyed, it must still be possible for the branches of humanity to physically communicate, despite the large distances and the supposed limit given by the speed of light. There is indeed reason to assume that intergalactic communication is already happening, both active and passive. If, for example, every form has something like a morphogenetic field, it could be possible for our subconscious mind to 'receive' images over large distances, that are in our day interpreted as 'mystical' or as 'fantasy.' If we however cannot refute the phenomenon of parapsychological images or visions as mere defects of the mind, the messages of morphogenetic fields offer a perfectly rational explanation. Apart from the trans-temporal and trans-spatial influence of morphogenetic fields there is more evidence for communication throughout space:

According to Sir Fred Hoyle, the evolution of humanity is determined by 'cosmic genes' that alter the human genes by combining their own DNA with that of the human gene! These cosmic genes are part of interstellar viruses that travel through space in a dried state, before they enter the Earth's atmosphere. Our genetic potential is, according to Professor Hoyle, continually modified by the genes of these space-travelling viruses. It seems therefore, that intergalactic communication is not achieved by the technological means of space-rockets, but by biological means, specifically by genes! On a cosmic scale, these genes are of course more comparable with particles whose job it is to convey and interrelate the information held by the actual genes, which account for forty-six planetary branches of the human race. The fact of communication between genes is physically established as far as a pair of chromosomes is concerned, since each chromosome pair is linked up by a physical connection that allows for an exchange of information from one chromosome to its symmetrical counterpart. In regard of this evidence, the Cosmic Egg Theory predicts the existence of extra-terrestrial human beings that have evolved from the same cosmic seed that is our own source of existence. Our longing for communication with these parallel branches of humanity, which is taken very seriously by NASA in various costly projects, is an expression of this genetic reality which provides for an information exchange between the otherwise unconnected bits of genetic storage in the Cosmic Egg. A possible contact with other members of the human race in this universe may not be a matter of distance or speed at all, but there may be a natural provision for contact to occur at regular intervals. If the genes from space, that constantly alter our evolutionary path, are not just another coincidence, but instead follow a natural pattern, we could perhaps learn to read their genetic code and thus consciously receive messages that we may have received for thousands of years on but a subconscious level. That the cosmic genes are intimately related to the human genes is sufficiently evinced by their ability to combine with the human DNA. Viruses causing physical malfunction (disease), obviously change our psychological well-being momentarily, and often leave us 'never quite the same.' The relationship between physical illness and psychological maladjustment seems to confirm the influence of viruses on our evolution. Since the evolution of humankind as a whole depends on all the chromosomes in the ovum, the evidence of genetic influence from space is highly confirmative of this proposed theory.

If we draw further comparisons, we notice that the periodic influence of cosmic genes goes along with an evolution that proceeds in jumps rather than gradually. The 'jump' from Neanderthal Man to Cro-Magnon Man for example was, just as the technological jumps of this century, not at all a consequence of gradual mutation and selection, but occurred rather suddenly. Also the evolutionary progress achieved by 'inventions,' like that of electricity or of the computer, happens in such jumps. Very often the 'new idea' occurs to several scientists at the same time, or in subconscious states like the dream-state. Such 'coincidences' cannot be explained by random events or by gradual mutation, but they can well be a consequence of sudden and periodic cosmic influences that are received by many people, but intuitively understood only by a few 'inventors.'

Further intensive research on genetics will eventually answer these questions in a definite and quantitative way, and should give us a better perspective of the microcosmic galaxies that make up DNA. As we learn to see evolution as a hierarchical function of embryology, which obeys the dualistic mechanics of the human form, the original question for the origin, the absolute beginning of the universe, and of humankind changes.

Aquina's idea that a creation event requires a cause is only correct in a limited sense, but has little relevance biologically or metaphysically. The creation of new life, just like the creation of the universe, can never be an original 'first move,' nor can life be caused by any-thing except life! Life has no absolute beginning, but existed long before this physical universe was even conceived. Creation can be understood only as a continuum without beginning or end, where causality is relevant only relative to very limited observers, and within each cyclical repetition. As far as this particular universe is concerned, the 'original' creation event is the event of conception, or in physical terms—the beginning of expansion towards the maximum point of its form. It does however make little sense to speak of an original creation event here, when every other creation event is just as original. Creation has not happened on day one, sometime in the past, but it is happening continuously, every day, when a seed starts to germinate, or when a baby is conceived, or a chemical reaction occurs. These events are just as original as the beginning of the universe, and the only difference is one of hierarchical scale. In our attempt to understand the origin of life and of the universe we should therefore study the creation events that happen daily before our eyes, and that hold all the answers for the creation events on larger scales.

If we want to learn about the large, so goes the opposite principle, it is best to first study the small!

When we ask ourselves the questions—where we come from, who we are and where we are going—we don't need to explore the far corners and the first seconds of the universe. The universe is far too large and remote for that. Our unique opportunity to understand the universe and its secrets, without any need for space-travel or for more advanced mathematical concepts, consists in our own minds and bodies, which are an exact microscopic mirror of the larger realities.

To become conscious of Self is therefore to be aware of all creation, just as Buddhism proclaims. In a hierarchically organized nature, the small must be contained in the large and form must reproduce itself, since the large is also contained in the small. This observation reduces spatial dimensions to a qualitative irrelevancy—and the Human Form becomes the only possible universe that contains every-thing there is to know.

Fractal contraction of the human body happens on many levels within the reproductive polarity of mature form and gene. So can iridology (iris diagnosis) acquire knowledge of the entire human system by examining the human iris, which is its microcosmic equivalent! The ear has been discovered to represent the embryo in its prenatal position, and the feet relate to all the inner organs on a contracted plane—which is used by acupuncture to influence the larger reality.

The reason why the universe is comprehensible is therefore far from mystical! The larger realities of the universe can be understood by their hierarchical symmetries in the human body and by the galaxies of matter we are. The microcosmic realities of our thought-processes, of the genes, and the information represented by genes on the other hand, are also the microcosmic reality of the physical universe which we can thus not only understand, but influence and create and be.

Each of our thoughts and attempts to understand the universe—changes the universe by changing its microcosmic structure in our brains!

Understanding any-thing means always understanding ourselves first, and there cannot in principle be any-thing to understand that we cannot find within ourselves. The Cosmic Embryo is thus the only all-inclusive system capable of contracting universal understanding into the human mind—and the human form is the only key in theory and daily life that fits the door to the mysteries of the physical and metaphysical universe. It is the only stage, where Mind and matter meet as a Oneness, and where the complexity of forms is reunited in simplicity and perfect symmetry.

22.The physical—metaphysical paradox

When considering the many contradictory and paradoxical theories on nature and the origin of Creation we find that the concept of the Cosmic Egg utterly unties this paradoxical knot of conflicting opposites by using every piece of the cosmic puzzle to arrive at a simple and complete theory that leaves nothing to coincidence! The complexity of forms and forces can, as we have seen, be comprehensibly explained in terms of life and by the mechanics of duality which is intrinsic to the Oneness of form.

The full validity of a system, including a scientific one, can however, as Kurt Goedel states in his second incompleteness theory, not be demonstrated within that system itself.

To explore the entire wealth of psychological and parapsychological factors contained in legends, spiritual teachings, dreams and altered states of mind, and to point out their close correspondence with the physical descriptions of the Cosmic Egg, would go beyond the tight scope of this outline of a new universal paradigm, and can be explored separately in the future. At this point we shall concentrate on only the most essential metaphysical descriptions that reflect the subconscious contents of the human psyche over thousands of years, and which have been held totally separate from any physical descriptions and scientific concepts for all this time. Throughout history, this world's religions have opposed each other over their claim of exclusive truth, and they have opposed science for the same reason and depicted it as demystifying and heretic. Theology and physics were worlds apart and could never confirm or relate to each other's reality. The incompleteness of each theory or system always led to doubt concerning its truth, and our history is thus filled with conflict, war, and other duality-battles. A complete theory however has to realize that great truth can never be either physical or metaphysical, and generally that logic does not require a decision of either/or! A fundamental law in this universe is the hierarchical coexistence of complexity and Oneness, where the One contains all of the many. Therefore, something which is One in itself, does not logically exclude the reality of the many. A dualistic logic however fails to realize this simple truth! If something is limited, so logic tells us, it cannot at the same time be unlimited. This conclusion is incorrect and shows the limitedness of our open-ended logic, which seems unable in principle to deal with Oneness and thus with unification. The only workable logic is that which reflects nature herself, and particularly the interconnected character of nature, where causality is cyclically reversible, and where duality is not a paradox, but the mechanics of the One.

A cyclical logic realizes that limitedness and boundlessness are not only compatible within a natural system, but also that one cannot be thought without the other. After all, something which is unlimited cannot be thought to be without a limit, because this would be a limitation in itself. Unlimited can simply only be—what has also a limit. The same logic applies to the question of whether nature is continuous or discontinuous. Evolutionary processes have no absolute beginning and no final end, but many beginnings and ends, and move in a continuous spiral of growing and disintegrating forms. Evolution is not gradual, but happens in quantum jumps where each phase comes to an abrupt end, only to give rise to another phase which is similarly discontinuous. Each step nature takes on her endless walk is like an idea that suddenly emerges out of nowhere and does not really continue from the last step. Every step is a new beginning and an end, but the movement at large is still continuous. Only what can end, can also continue, and every-thing that will live forever must also die.

The opposite principle applies to every paradox, including that of a differentiation between the physical and the metaphysical. Physics and metaphysics are actually only two different modes of contemplating the same reality. Just as the natural and physical unknown has regularly been perceived as supernatural and metaphysical before it was explained physically, so can we expect our metaphysical God to be a natural phenomenon that can be described physically. Metaphysical and physical reality are simply not two different things, but aspects of the One that is metaphysical but also physical. This means that God, described as metaphysical by physics and described as physical by all religions, cannot be the unexplainable Tao of Lao-tzu! We cannot describe or even attempt to explain the unexplainable. What we can discern as the Almighty Creator, as the omnipresent and eternal One God with a deep connection to humanity, is still a metaphysical God. It is however a physical God also, and it has to be, if only in order to be unlimited. This metaphysical God, described as the One by religion, transcends the paradoxes of duality and of causal logic and is clearly the One in whose image we are created! The God of the religions is not, as too easily assumed, the unexplainable Tao, but a God that has been described in much detail as the Father, the Son, the spirit, the Mother, the state of mind, the destroyer and the creator and yes, as the baby born to be man—and becoming God! The fact, that God is generally pictured in the human form, male and female, can of course be interpreted psychologically and need not have any significance. It is however otherwise if the human psyche relates to reality at all! The old man with the white beard need not be the primitive or naive concept for what we see it today, when God has to be a 'pure consciousness' or 'pure love,' or at least something well beyond the laws of physics. The old man can actually be a physical reality! In our intellectual time, a personalized God does not fit our abstract concepts of infinity and boundlessness very well, because the human form is seen as limited and flawed and destined to die, and cannot seem to account for the vastness of space. The ancients would however have considered our logic as equally primitive, since a truly unlimited God can logically exist not only beyond the boundaries of personal manifestation, but necessarily within these boundaries as well.

If a transcendental God cannot be manifest as a person, like the old man with the beard or the Cosmic Mother—this God is not unlimited. This is probably what the ancients felt intuitively, and it is what children and simple people feel, to whom any complicated and abstract metaphysical concept of God is something they cannot and will not relate to. God has to include all abstract and also all personal qualities we ever conceived of in order to live up to all our metaphysical expectations. Thus, it makes no difference whether a little girl prays fervently to the virgin Mary or whether another child dances in the honour of Krishna. God is every-thing and nothing and the intellectuals can never be closer to God than the 'poor in spirit.' If the metaphysical God is unlimited enough to also be a person, there can be nothing primitive about the descriptions of religion that stubbornly claim that God is manifest in the human form.

These descriptions of God, quite similar in all religions, are what we need to compare with the physical descriptions of the Cosmic Egg Theory, to see if there really remains any unsolvable paradox or a logical contradiction which would continue to separate the physical from the metaphysical theories of reality. The first description of God we are looking at is the duality of asserting the existence of God, which is to be a gnostic—and doubting it, which is to be an agnostic.

To doubt that the God of religion is the final, unexplainable God, or the Tao, is very justified, and considering the dogmatism with which the religions demand faith in their limited concepts, it is almost necessary to become an agnostic if only to keep an open mind and to admit one's own ignorance. This is where the agnostic often recognizes truth, while the believer ceases to seek the truth, thinking he found it already. On the other hand, the agnostic overlooks that life, love and God are not to be asserted or denied, but to be experienced! To observe the beauty and perfection of Creation and to allow the inner Self to respond to it, is to become a gnostic—one who knows. The agnostic and the gnostic both recognize valid parts of the truth, and one could say that being an agnostic and a gnostic at the same time would be perfect because once we learn that we know nothing, we have learned the real thing. In any case, both the gnostic and the agnostic have a concept of God, which they either accept or refute and this concept includes at least the experience of life which cannot be denied. Many religions, including those asserting the existence of the One God are inclined to describe not only their godhead, but also the physical principles and the principles of life as relating to God. The main emphasis is always given to the dualistic nature of Creation, and to the either/or paradoxes of life that have only been explained in terms of God. The importance of duality, as the link between the physical world of the many forms, and the 'transcendental' idea of Oneness, is most clearly expressed by the concept of Yin and Yang in Asian mysticism. This concept holds that there are only two forces which account for every change in the universe—the expanding force and the contracting force.

In Hinduism, this general principle is set against a background where God takes on a split personality to emphasize on the significance of Yin and Yang for Creation. The creative process in Hinduism is not a linear evolution towards a goal, but is symbolized by Vishnu, the Creator, and Shiva, the destroyer. To comprehend Creation (expansion) as linked with destruction (contraction) shows intuitive understanding for an as-well-as duality, and for its relevance to the perception of reality and of Oneness. Closely related to the duality of expansion/contraction as the creative principle is another duality in Hinduism which has also to do with creation.

The tantric duality of Vishnu/Parvati or Rama/Sita as divine lovers is the most ubiquitous sculpture in Indian temples and the most lovingly expressed image of all—where the act of love and of conception becomes the highest principle and expression of the divine, and the path to Oneness and enlightenment. One cannot help but notice the direct correspondence of these theological descriptions with the physical descriptions of the cosmic egg universe.

In Buddhism, the One God is the conscious, undivided human Self that has achieved Oneness by transcending the paradoxes of duality! This extract from an old text from the Zen-masters illustrates the key importance of duality for the relationship between the physical and the metaphysical reality in Buddhist thinking:

A tenth of an inch's difference, and heaven and earth are set apart,

If you wish to see it before your own eyes, have no fixed thoughts either for or against it.

When you strive to gain quiescence by stopping motion,

The quiescence thus gained is ever in motion,

As long as you tarry in the dualism,

How can you realize Oneness?

And when Oneness is not thoroughly understood,

In two ways loss is sustained:

The denying of reality is the asserting of it,

And the asserting of emptiness is the denying of it.

If an eye never falls asleep,

All dreams will by themselves cease:

If the Mind retains its absoluteness,

The ten thousand things are of one

Suchness. In the higher realm of true Suchness

There is neither 'self' nor 'other:' When direct identification is sought, we can only say, 'Not two.'

In being 'not two' all is the same,

All that is, is comprehended in it;

The wise in the ten quarters they all enter into this Absolute Reason.

This Absolute Reason is beyond quickening (time) and extending (space),

For it one instant is ten thousand years, whether we see it or not, it is manifest everywhere in all the ten quarters.

Infinitely small things are as large as large things can be,

For here no external conditions obtain;

Infinitely large things are as small as small things can be,

For objective limits are here of no consideration.

What is, is the same as what is not, what is not is the same as what is:

Where this state of things fails to obtain,
Indeed no tarrying there.
One in All, All in One-If only this is realized,
No more worry about your not being perfect!

The emphasis of Asian mysticism on the possibility to achieve Oneness by transcending the paradoxes of twoness, can be found in most or all metaphysical systems.

For instance—Thomas, Log. 22: Jesus said to them:

If you make two into one and the inside as the outside, the above as the below, and if you make the male and the female into One, so that the male is not male and the female not female...then you will enter the Kingdom.

Christianity hints at the principle of mutually attractive polarities with most Jesus-words like: 'The last will be the first.' He speaks about the God who is born as man to become God once again. Just as in Hinduism, God is not a purely metaphysical God, but goes through cycles of rebirth, on the physical plane, thus becoming man. The birth of God as man and the resurrection of the man as a God are the two pillars of Christianity—and if taken literally, they describe the physical existence of God within a cycle of birth and rebirth, where God becomes man and man becomes God. The prophecy, that Jesus is going to return, explains that the cycle God-Man-God is not a single event, but the fundamental principle, relating God to man—as it is also confirmed by the reincarnations of God in the Asian religions. This brings us to the question of whether the One God can reincarnate as the many Gods and still be one God. The paradox of the One God and the many Gods is recognized as a great mystery by Buddhism, Hinduism and Christianity. The Christian 'Holy Trinity' of the Father, the Son and the Holy Spirit is like the multiple Gods of Hinduism an example of how the One God is not seen as exclusively One, but as including the various aspects of the many. If we want to see the whole picture to which all theological descriptions contribute valuable parts, we only need to assemble the various puzzle pieces and realize that what we call mystery is easily understood in physical and biological terms.

If the 'Holy Trinity' describes the One God (The Human Form) as the Father and the Son and the Spirit, we must surely realize, that the Mother has been left out of the real picture! Since most ancient religions emphasized the Mother as the supreme Goddess of all creation, this omission is understandable, since Christianity, as the most jealously exclusive of religions, had to avoid any recognition of 'primitive' or 'pagan' Gods. The truth, having a way of re-emerging from suppression, did however adjust this picture later, when the virgin Mary, the 'Mother of God,' invaded Christianity and became the possibly most revered aspect of the One God once again.

The tantric acts of love and conception between the humanoid Gods of Hinduism may appear as very different from Christian chastity and sin and 'immaculate conception' from a moral perspective. But the essential point of the story remains always the same: God, the Human Form, manifests in pairs of male and female, is united in the act of love, and reproduces genetically, eventually resulting in the birth of a new God—the Son! Christ made it quite explicit that he was the Son of God—and our brother—and that we were all sisters and brothers, meaning, with some logic applied, that humanity as a whole is the Son of God! Therefore, as Christ pointed out, every act we commit against our neighbor is also done against himself, or God. The bible and the Veda are filled with such explicit details that have never been considered to apply both in a metaphysical, symbolic sense and also in the obvious and physical or biological sense they explicitly express! This is because the mysteries of the unknown have never been thought capable of including the known physical realities. One cannot be any clearer than to say: 'Man is created in the image of God.' If our mystical ideas of God were not so artificially separated from the real, physical world, it would have been very easy to receive the obvious message that man, being the Son of God, is therefore created in God's image!

The God of the religions on one hand, and humanity on the other, are thus related in a way that describes the cyclical continuation of the Human Form within the spatial Hierarchy as propelled by sexual reproduction.

The metaphysical God is in this way never only 'beyond' physics—but always also within physics. Physics and biology describe in their limited way not what God has created in the past, but what God is doing at present! Genetics may seem to us like just another limited concept, but really it is very much the basic principle that unifies all physical phenomena. Genes determine the mechanics of the creative process itself; they are the tool in the hands of every God.

Genetics is the clay from which God made man in His/Her image! If Creation at large can only be recognized by the small creation events on our scale, we shouldn't be surprised at the discovery that God acts inside physics as well as outside of it. Physics and biology carefully describe how God creates God physically, while philosophy and psychology describe how God creates God consciously. Conventional science will of course never detect a truly original 'first move,' an absolute beginning of any causal relationship, or a first beginning of life as long as it is looking for absolute beginnings somewhere in the past. Only in the here and now can a beginning be properly observed! But there is never any absolute beginning. Every time we watch a seed germinate, we are facing as new a creation as can ever be, and we are also watching the Creator at work—and a universe expand! This can however not be easily understood as long as we define God as the Creator only, but not as the Creation. Physically, a God who is the first cause and the Creator of a creation seems to make sense as far as this God obeys our causal, open-ended logic. A metaphysical God however has to be beyond the logic of causality, since He/She is supposed to be unlimited and eternal! A God who is only cause and not effect would be limited and psychologically motivated to create what he somehow needs—and thus fall short of what we are able to expect metaphysically. When we seek the truth, particularly the metaphysical kind, we need to realize that truth does not mean a decision between the existing logical alternatives. A metaphysical truth does not ever require that its opposite be excluded from equal consideration. It must rather describe a reality which includes the various alternative views hitherto, and it should show how the seemingly conflicting descriptions can combine and fall in place to become compatible parts of a larger, unifying explanation.

A philosophy of as-well-as needs to replace our philosophies of either-or!

Only as a consequence of our dualistic reason, everything seems to need a beginning and an end. It needs to be good or bad, right or wrong. The absolute truth however includes always both, otherwise it is only a limited observation leading to opinions and to dogma! It is because our Gods are conceived as limited, causal agencies, that they exclude the Gods of others who simply have a different type of limitation. This theory proposes a completely unifying concept of God that does not exclude any other theological concept! The One God, in order to achieve consistency with all experience, and to be congruent with Her/His microcosmic mirror-image, has to be the human form itself. Naturally, the human form as an abstract concept is a Oneness and so is any human individual. From an embryonic point of view however, the aspects of the Father and the Mother (or duality), and of Self are three indispensable aspects of the One—just as we cannot help but receive a triangle when we reconnect three points. This is what the Holy Trinity of Christianity and the Asian idea of 'Self' are trying to express. God to us is One—the 'Self' —but there is also the Mother and the Father!

The question of whether the One God is male or female is the wrong question, also imposed by the dualistic confinements of our either/or logic. The One God has to be both male and female. There is no paradox and no mystery. The human Self also comes in pairs of male and female, so how could God not be both? As far as the cosmic Self in the Egg is concerned, this God has to be male! Confirmation for the cosmic embryo being male is given by all the major religious traditions. Jesus, Buddha, Mohammed, Krishna, Zarathustra, Bodhidarma—are all male! Representing the Embryo (mankind), these avatars or prophets point into the future and lead the way for humankind to follow! The influence of these men on our psychological evolution has been tremendous and certainly not random. The reason, why the major religions today are more dominant than the ones emphasizing other aspects of God, like the sun or the water, can be found in that focus on the aspect of the 'Son,' to whom humans can relate more directly the more they become aware of their collective selves and of unity. Christianity describes the existence of the Father, the Mother of God, and of the Son quite correctly, and emphasizes on the birth of God as man, who again becomes God (showing the path, the truth and the life). It tells us that we were created in the image of God, that we are all brothers and sisters of each other and of Christ, who represents the Son of God. Very clear words.

The Celts and most ancient cultures emphasized the Mother and the event of child-birth over the hierarchical components of God—water, fire, emptiness, breath or earth. The divine duality, which in Asia is the male yang and the female yin, has the same significance to the Celts who saw the universe as controlled by the force of the bull (expanding force) and the female force of the horse (contracting force), where the horse, Epona, is at the same time the Mother Goddess. It should be pointed out, as a matter of interest, that the remarkable Pablo Picasso used the bull and the horse as his leading motives, expressing consistently the magic of duality. It was Picasso's druidic vision, more than his craft, that made him so knowing and so capable of relating the mysteries through images of the physical. When we can't decide how to identify what all cultures for thousands of years have called 'the Mother,' we can look at Picasso's many faces of women, one more enlightening than the other—and see each as a part of the divine woman in Picasso's vision. Whether the Mother is addressed as the Celtic Epona, or as the Hindu Goddess Parvati, as Kali, Gaia, the Earth Mother, as Mary, or as the Cosmic Mother who reunites them all—the basic fact is always the same, and the descriptions vary only relative to cultural influence.

Asian tradition tells us, that the One God is the Self and that all life forms are one, but controlled by the forces of Yin and Yang, which account for the existence of the many phenomena. This same description is given by most religions, only in different words. Also, the Gods of the various religions are always the same, different only in name, not in significance. So basically, all religions describe the same reality; they all relate God with the physical world and with the Human Form, but they emphasize those aspects that their culture can best identify with. There may be slight differences in the teachings on how to achieve Godhood, even where the descriptions of God themselves are not at all contradictory, but overwhelmingly corroborating. The same thing can be said for many cosmological statements by Greek philosophers.

So did Anaximander, who believed in the 'innumerable worlds,' actually identify those with gods who came into being, rising and passing away at long intervals—a theory that was never taken seriously!

The New Zealand Maori have a God who is understood as the Embryo. This God, Tiki, is responsible for all creation...

What about the philosophy of materialism, then? Is it the only concept that will remain incompatible with the metaphysical physics of the Cosmic Egg? One we must condemn? As far as materialism claims that there can be no causal factor beside matter, it is certainly as limited as any exclusive dogmatic system. But on the other hand, it is not actually wrong to see matter as a real and important phenomenon of Creation, especially since physical matter provides the observable plane for us from which alone we can venture into questions about more transcendental realities. Matter contains and reveals the design of life, and the study of matter is our best path to the discovery of Mind. Thus, materialism can be appreciated as a down to Earth method that, according to the principle of mutually attractive opposites, starts to explore the opposite of Mind in order to in time arrive at Mind itself. After all, we have to bend our knees before jumping up. . . Materialism is grounding, and it is no more removed from the spiritual than the body (and brain) is from mind. And God, after all, is physical as well! However—as far as materialism does not recognize the duality between Mind and matter, it is not capable to explain reality in a comprehensible way and it stalls at the newest discoveries of quantum physics that show that matter comes in probabilistic indeterminacies that are influenced by the mind of the observer. Just like any exclusive philosophy, materialism describes only one side of the coin—but like all other philosophies it confirms the existence and the nature of the coin itself from its own perspective.

To reveal the metaphysical descriptions offered by religion as a physical reality may seem demystifying to many religious people, as far as their Gods are thus 'reduced' to physical entities. One must however bear in mind, that relative to humankind on our scale, the Cosmic Mother, or God the Father, actually fit our traditional definitions of a God very well. But the mature cosmic human form is of course billions of years more evolved than us, or any of the humanoid 'gods' that may have visited the Greek. The Cosmic God is a transcendental God in every sense. The Cosmic Mother is 'almighty' in an absolute sense, is the creator of this universe and omnipresent in each part of it. The Human Form is not only the spirit permeating all known existence (the Holy Spirit), where according to the animists everything has a soul—but our bread and wine are indeed the flesh and blood of God, as is the whole universe!

Another physically explainable mystery is the idea of a 'heaven,' where we can be conscious of God, reunited with our loved ones and live forever. Heaven can be physically the location of the Cosmic God after birth, but spiritually it is the state of becoming conscious of the Oneness of all things and thus becoming part of the future divine consciousness. Heaven is a state of mind, but it is also a place. A common human misconception is to fear for the metaphysical nature of God when the unknown is suddenly found to be explainable in physical terms. Why can God and the mystery of life not be recognized within the physical reality of every-day life?

The paradox of physics/metaphysics is the paradox of matter/mind, and it is the hardest one to dissolve, despite the fact, that we ourselves are body and mind in one! Despite the fact that every cell in our bodies contains genes, memories, perception, and the blue-print for the whole system, we still locate the Mind in our brains and artificially separate it from the rest of the body. While medicine tries to understand the physical body independently of the mind, psychology tries to deal with the mind without relating it to its physical manifestation—and thus both systems remain mysterious, separated and incomplete. This differentiation between mind and matter is found on every level of human thought, including physics, and it is the reason why quantum physics is so surprising and difficult to accept. If we examine the smallest building-blocks of matter, the particles, we can simply not find any solid and definite reality that would fit our definitions of what is matter. Instead we discover that particles can be described as waves, or as energy, or as mere possibilities or probabilities for actual being, depending on the method we use to observe and measure them and think about them. Particles cannot be identified individually, but only as groups that behave according to a probabilistic pattern. The point is that when we observe a probabilistic event, it changes the outcome of the experiment, and when we don't observe it, the phenomenon itself ceases to exist. Matter is thus on its basic levels a function of mind, and has no separate existence apart from mind! In the same way, physics has no relevance of its own, but is a function of the metaphysical aspect of consciousness. One could say, that the wave-character of the subatomic particles relates to their particle-character, as brain-waves relate to the physical world. In other words—consciousness itself has a double nature. It is wave-like and it is particle-like. In again other words—form itself is particle-like and wave-like, because light, which is a property of form, connects form with the dimensions of space-time by the means of its wave-character. This is why an 'objective' observer creates the 'observation' that without him would not exist.

In an infinite universe, the possibility of the quantum phenomenon 'particle' to be actualized is enough to send a (brain-) wave into the direction and precise position of our experiment where we consciously or subconsciously expect to see a comprehensible or probabilistic pattern. Naturally, we will still detect the deposited quantum of the wave, but we also have a materialized outcome of the influence our observations have exerted on the probabilistic potential of the particle-structure, copying the image our mind composes, responding to the mind—looking into a mirror. A more detailed explanation for how mind and matter are identical is demonstrated by the geometry of harmonics, an exploration of which would exceed our limited scope here.

When it is recognized that the cosmic Mind determines the probability patterns of quantum events—how can then physics be separate from metaphysics and how can matter be distinguished from mind?

We are living at a point in time, where our scientific logic has started to become aware of its dualistic confinement. Quantum mechanics gives us no choice at all over whether matter consists of either particles or waves, and nature gives us no real choice of whether we like to see ourselves as the body or as the mind. The philosophy of either/or will die in the West, just as it has died to a good degree in the East a long time ago. We are learning that duality defines and arises from the principle of Oneness, and that mind and matter are but two aspects of being, as the wave-character and the particle-character of matter are just two aspects of reality. Once we have started to transcend the paradoxes of our linear logic, we can redefine our methods of observation and describe reality in a more complete way. The observer, explaining the reality of observables from which he is separate (or thinks he is), can only really explain his own method, his instruments, and his point of view—by the metaphors of his own mind. Reality cannot directly be described for a system other than Self. Only when the observer and the observed are One, can reality be directly perceived. This act of observation must necessarily be subjective at that stage. The end of paradox, of dualistic logic, of linear cause and effect, and of the differentiation between physics and philosophy seems to indicate an end to science as we know it, and an end to our faith in tangible reality. Certainly, we will have to redefine reality in terms of the mind, and science will need to redefine relationships between events in a multi-causal way. But is this really the end of science? Does the existence of the mind exclude the reality of matter? Or is it not rather that an understanding of paradox gives us back the full reality of phenomena that previously were indeterminate?

When Creation is comprehended as both aggregation and disintegration, and Self is recognized as both mind and matter—do we then not stand at the very beginning of a new science, capable of dealing with the 'Ding an sich' rather than with disconnected coordinates?

A creation, perceived as both limited and unlimited, both material and conscious, both physical and metaphysical, can now be explored in new ways, as far as its mechanics are concerned. We can still describe matter in terms of waves or fields and in terms of particles, and we can still understand the universe as a wave, a field, a geometric pattern of harmonics, and as a solid physical body. All these descriptions are valid since every description creates the aspect it discovers by projecting it. There is nothing unreal about this discovery/creation process. Only, we cannot continue to be exclusive about any description, and we need to be conscious of the fact that an observation or description often creates the very thing we observe. We are no longer just predicting the future, but we are building it! And we are totally responsible for all that happens!

A new science will not try and explore a vast universe from one end of an imaginary scale to the other, nor need any 'evolution' to explain the expanding phase of a single oscillation of the human form, but it will conclusively understand the mechanics of duality, which is the vehicle of the cyclical continuation of Oneness (form), and which places all the known forces into a comprehensible context. The physical forces can be directly related to the design, to the forms contained by the Mind, and to the waves produced by the Mind.

The end of orthodox science does not mean that the universe can now only be described in terms of the mind, in waves or ideas. After all, the brain waves and ideas (forms, archetypes) are always also physical things! Every end is a new beginning, and a physical-metaphysical unification cannot deny the wonders of the physical side of reality. Even if the universe is a wave and a field and an illusion, it is also a solid physical phenomenon, or more precisely the physical expression of Mind. To explore this universe, we but have to explore our own mind and our own bodies, since the universe is as much a mirror-image of our body as it is of human consciousness. If physics describes the physical reality of the universe as a growing human body, philosophy describes it as the growing human self-awareness. In this way, all paradoxes are simultaneously resolved, as much within physics and biology as within philosophy, as between all systems. The study of the universe becomes the study of its fractal—man!

Physics, psychology, philosophy, anthropology, mathematics, geometry, and all other branches of human thought serve this same purpose—the study of Self by the Self! The exploration of Self, to which we are inexorably driven by the implications of quantum physics, will prove to be the ultimate foundation of scientific study. The way we see the universe is the way we, the observer, really are—as we decide the probabilistic outcome of our projections and experiments! The observer of our scale becomes the Creator on the quantum level! God has indeed not played dice, when She gave life to humankind and to the universe—and neither can we play dice, while we continue to create in our own image!

We cannot choose to play dice when deciding whether we are the body or the mind, but if we do, this choice will immediately distort our perception. Beyond the duality of choice, we are simply both—body and mind. Thus, we don't throw the dice, but create reality as it creates itself. Fate and free choice are ultimately identical—and we are predetermined because we must determine ourselves before we can fully become who we are.

Our body (the brain) physically conducts the processes of the mind, and the mind conducts the quantum processes of matter, without there being any actual boundary between the two. There is, in principle, no way to objectively differentiate between body and mind, since they are truly one and the same thing. The human consciousness, (the human form) is as much a metaphysical phenomenon as it is a physical one, a chemical, biological, philosophical and psychological one—all at the same time. By emphasizing the mechanistic and specialized aspects of science for so long, we have now moved towards the opposite—discovering how much more alive and simple reality is, and how nothing can ever be understood in isolation of every-thing else. Now, that we have discovered the importance of the mind, we can go forward into a new physics and explore the physical manifestations of Mind, no longer searching for a metaphysical Creator in the past or beyond physics, but here and now! We know, that we can experience God in the here and now through all of our many senses. Thus, we will quantum-leap to discover the incredible truth about ourselves, and we will take a step deeper into the Oneness that is in the recognition of Self by the Self, the awareness in man—of God.

Other books by Fritz Blackburn:

-Travel-parenting: https://books2read.com/u/mlGEYM

- Chess-parenting - How to Significantly Increase Your Child's IQ: https://books2read.com/u/3yp2yL

- Reality and Shit: https://books2read.com/u/3kweBR

- Goddess Unleashed - About Sacred Sex, Filipina Goddesses, and Witches: **https://www.smashwords.com/books/view/2017305**

-**Tuko's Cave:** https://www.smashwords.com/books/view/1639042

- **The Brink of Becoming** - Designing a Future beyond Zionism and Cultural Programming: **https://www.smashwords.com/books/view/2011620**

Also by Fritz Blackburn

The Cosmic Egg
Reality and Shit
Travel Parenting
Tuko's Cave
The Brink of Becoming - Designing a Future beyond Zionism and
Cultural Programming
Goddess Unleashed - About Sacred Sex, Filipina Goddesses, and
Witches
Ursprung, Wesen und Absicht des lebenden Universums

About the Author

Fritz Blackburn lives with his wife Ikay in New Zealand, surrounded by native bush and wildlife. He has studied law, economics and psychology in his hometown Augsburg in Bavaria and then lived in remote cultures all over the world. He speaks 8 languages, is a master chessplayer, a tantric and spiritual teacher, and nature lover.